AMAZING L'NU'K

WORDS BY JULIE PELLISSIER-LUSH
AND ROBIN GRANT

ART BY JAMES BENTLEY

NIMBUS
PUBLISHING
— NIMBUS.CA —

TO ALL MI'KMAW CHILDREN FROM THE PAST, PRESENT, AND FUTURE— WE RESPECT YOU, WE LOVE YOU, AND WE SEE HOW AMAZING YOU ARE. WE CELEBRATE YOU WITHIN THESE PAGES, AND ALWAYS WITHIN OUR HEARTS.

Nimbus Publishing Limited
3660 Strawberry Hill Street, Halifax, NS, B3K 5A9
(902) 455-4286 nimbus.ca
Printed and bound in Canada
NB1622
Interior design: Peggy Issenman, Peggy & Co. Design, and Jenn Embree
Cover design: Jenn Embree/Heather Bryan
Editor: Penelope Jackson
Editor for the press: Claire Bennet

Library and Archives Canada Cataloguing in Publication
Title: Amazing l'nu'k : a celebration of the people of Mi'kma'ki /
words by Julie Pellissier-Lush & Robin Grant ; art by James Bentley.
Names: Pellissier-Lush, Julie, 1970- author. | Grant, Robin (Author), author. | Bentley, James, 1968- illustrator.
Description: Includes bibliographical references.
Identifiers: Canadiana (print) 20220473137 | Canadiana (ebook) 20220473315 | ISBN 9781774711682 (softcover) | ISBN 9781774711699 (EPUB)
Subjects: CSH: Mi'kmaq—Biography. | LCGFT: Biographies.
Classification: LCC E99.M6 P45 2023 | DDC 920.0092/97343—dc23

Nimbus Publishing acknowledges the financial support for its publishing activities from the Government of Canada, the Canada Council for the Arts, and from the Province of Nova Scotia. We are pleased to work in partnership with the Province of Nova Scotia to develop and promote our creative industries for the benefit of all Nova Scotians.

TABLE OF CONTENTS

A NOTE FROM THE AUTHORS

In the spirit of Truth and Reconciliation, the research and writing within this book was conducted by activist and **Epekwitnewaq** Mi'kmaw poet laureate Julie Pellissier-Lush and accomplice educator and journalist Robin Grant. We, the authors, offer our deepest gratitude, **wela'liek**, to our many Mi'kmaw friends, allies, and colleagues who lent their time and expertise to this project. This work would never have been possible without your inspiration and support.

In keeping with the *Amazing Atlantic Canadians* series, we only feature a few select **L'nu'k** originally from or residing within the region currently known as "Atlantic Canada" in this book. We acknowledge the huge breadth and diversity of amazing L'nu'k who have lived and continue to live across all of Mi'kma'ki. We wish we could have written about all of you.

The Mi'kmaw translations found throughout this book, including spellings, pronunciations, place names—and the district names and their geographical boundaries—are based on our research. We recognize that spellings, pronunciations, translations, and knowledge may differ from community to community. In this case, we chose to use the Smith/Francis orthography for consistency. One of the most popular versions of how to spell and define the Mi'kmaw language, the Smith/Francis orthography is sort of like a Mi'kmaw dictionary that contains the spelling, meaning, and pronunciation of Mi'kmaw words. Our only exception to this rule occurs out of respect for the L'nu'k being profiled, in cases where they express strong family ties to the Listuguj orthography. Heavily influenced by the French colonial settlers, the Listuguj orthography is the next most popular way of communicating in Mi'kmaw.

Throughout the book Mi'kmaw words will appear in bold, and you can look them up in the glossary, starting on page 173.

Meanwhile, special thanks to Elder Gary Simon for his lifelong work as a Knowledge Keeper for the Mi'kmaw language and for proofing this text in particular. The authors also thank Nimbus Publishing for agreeing to pioneer and uphold OCAP® principles for the individuals profiled in this text. Developed by the First Nations Information Governance Centre, OCAP® Principles stand for the right of First Nations to fully own, control, access, and possess their respective community's information.

We thank all of those who suggest alternate spellings, pronunciations, translations, and knowledge, and ask for understanding as the Mi'kmaq Nation works to strengthen and grow together.

Last but not least, we thank all those who have supported us through this process: you know who you are! All these pages and stories are here because of you.

THE MI'KMAW TERRITORY

The territory of **Mi'kma'ki** includes all of Nova Scotia and Prince Edward Island, the Gaspé Peninsula of Quebec, eastern New Brunswick, and part of Newfoundland. It also extends down into Maine. The **Mi'kmaq** divide Mi'kma'ki into seven districts: Epekwitk aq Piktuk; Unama'kik aq Ktaqmkuk; Eskikewa'kik; Sipekne'katik; Kespukwitk; Siknikt; and Kespe'k. These are as follows:

Epekwitk aq Piktuk. When translated from Mi'kmaw to English, *Epekwitk* means "lying in the water." This area includes the entire province of Prince Edward Island. Meanwhile, *Piktuk* means "the explosive place," and is the area currently known as Pictou County, Nova Scotia. Both Epekwitk *aq* (and) Piktuk are considered one district.

Unama'kik aq Ktaqmkuk. Translated literally, *Unama'kik* means "foggy lands." This area consists of the entire island of Cape Breton, Nova Scotia. Meanwhile, *Ktaqmkuk* means "land across the water." This land mass represents the entire island of Newfoundland, and does not include Labrador.

Eskikewa'kik. In Mi'kmaw this means "skin-dresser's territory." This territory includes Guysborough and Halifax County, Nova Scotia, and all the land in between.

Sipekne'katik. This translates literally to "wild potato area," and consists of the city of Halifax as well as Indian Brook, New Ross, Pennal, Dodd, and counties Lunenburg, Kings, Hants, and Colchester, all in Nova Scotia.

Kespukwitk. In Mi'kmaw this means "last flow." This area is, again, just in Nova Scotia, and consists of the counties of Queens, Shelburne, Yarmouth, Digby, and Annapolis.

Siknikt. This Mi'kmaw word in English means "drainage area." The area is made up of Cumberland, Nova Scotia, as well as Westmorland, Albert, Kent, Saint John, Kings, and Queens Counties in New Brunswick.

Kespe'k. This Mi'kmaw word means "last land." This area consists of all the land north of Richibucto, New Brunswick, including parts of Gaspé, Quebec.

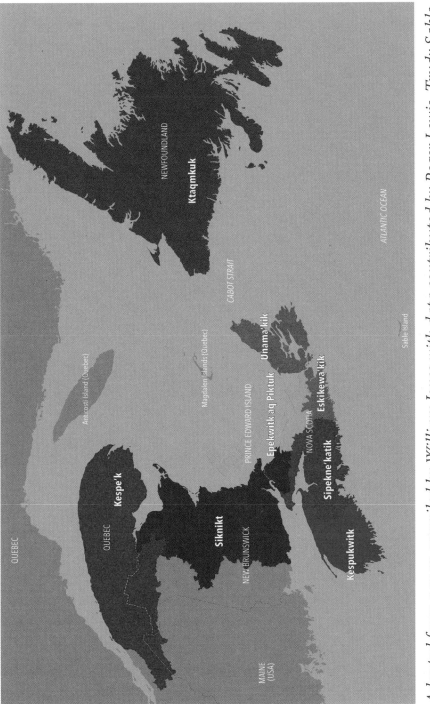

Adapted from a map compiled by William Jones with data contributed by Roger Lewis, Trudy Sable, and Bernie Francis.

The Mi'kmaw Territory

A BRIEF HISTORY OF MI'KMA'KI

Amazing people, or L'nu'k, the Mi'kmaq, were here in Mi'kma'ki since time immemorial (Mi'kma'ki includes the area called "Atlantic Canada" today, plus some parts of Maine and Quebec). While ancient fossils and artifacts prove the Mi'kmaq roamed these meadows and swam these lakes some thirteen thousand years ago, generations of preserved storytelling suggest they have been here much longer. That's long before the printing press, the Egyptian pyramids, the end of the Ice Age...even before the wheel was invented. Both carbon dating and **Mi'kmaw** oral history portray these first L'nu'k as nomadic hunters, fishers, and gatherers, settling in camps close to rivers and lakes to seek out fish, eels, and other water creatures in the summer and venturing inland during the cooler months to hunt large game.

When the first European explorers arrived by ship, beginning around the sixteenth century, the L'nu'k of Mi'kma'ki greeted them as friends. In fact, many scholars suggest the word for "my kin friends"—***Nikmaq*** in Mi'kmaw—is the origin of the word *Mi'kmaq* itself, given it was likely the first phrase these early settlers heard as they landed on the shores of Mi'kma'ki. In this same spirit of friendship, the Mi'kmaw and British Nations conducted a swift trade, and by the eighteenth century, established the Peace and Friendship Treaties. Through a series of legally binding agreements, the Mi'kmaq allowed the British to settle peacefully on their land, provided the Mi'kmaq could continue to go about their hunting, fishing, and harvesting as usual.

And while cruel attempts to force the Mi'kmaq and other Indigenous people to adopt colonial ways—such as forcing children to leave their homes and families, speak English, and attend residential schools—would forever change the destiny of all those who originally called Turtle Island home, many L'nu'k managed to maintain their culture, traditions, and language.

They did this through generations of storytelling. By keeping this longstanding tradition and their warrior spirit close to their hearts, they managed to stay strong, and never surrender or give up their lands. They made sure their language and traditions would never die.

And that's just part of what makes them so amazing.

TURTLE ISLAND

It might sound like some faraway island full of turtles, but it's actually what some Indigenous people, like the Mi'kmaq, call the continent of North America, while others, such as the Ojibwa, use "Turtle Island" to refer to the entire world. The name itself comes from various Indigenous oral histories that repeatedly tell the story of "a turtle that holds the whole world on its back."

IMPORTANT TERMS

hen the famous white colonialist Christopher Columbus first set sail from his Italian seaport in the late fifteenth century, his intention was always to explore *the Indies*—or the area known today as "Asia." Instead, he ended up here, on the shores of "North America," or as many Indigenous people prefer to call it, Turtle Island. Unaware of his mistake, he came to label the first people he encountered *Indian.*

The term *Indian* really stuck, like *for six hundred years* kind of stuck. It stuck even though it was always, in fact, incorrect. And while you may notice the term throughout these pages, in the names of some groups and government departments, or because some Indigenous people still choose to call themselves Indian, most prefer not to use the term at all. Because the term carries so much harmful history, it is not one that should ever be used outside of these special circumstances.

This is why we have chosen to use the term *Indigenous*—a word that describes those people who originally lived in a place. Otherwise, we will use the correct words to specifically describe those who are Indigenous to Mi'kma'ki (see also the Mi'kmaw Glossary of Terms on page 173):

❋ **L'nu** means "an individual who is Mi'kmaw."

❋ **Mi'kmaw** also means "L'nu," or "an individual who is Mi'kmaw." This word can also be used as an adjective (for example, "She is a Mi'kmaw woman").

❋ **L'nu'k** means "the Mi'kmaw people."

❋ **The Mi'kmaq** also means "L'nu'k," or "the Mi'kmaw people."

❋ **L'nuey** means "belonging to the L'nu'k/Mi'kmaq."

PART I

ACTIVISTS AND HEROES

As a Mi'kmaw, you're very proud to know that…we come from that long line of warriors and there are so many people who are willing to step up and protect our way of life and who we are, our human rights as Mi'kmaw people.

—Sma'knis and Former US Marine Corps Sergeant **Mike Stephens**, Millbrook First Nation

We are always asked, 'Can you provide documents that prove you are descended from the original Mi'kmaw treaty signees?' I always ask in return, 'Can you prove you are descended from John Cabot or someone here at that time?' I don't have to prove my continuity to anyone.

—Kji-keptin **Alexander Denny**, Eskasoni First Nation

Alton Gas needs to Google our history in upholding our treaty and our title. They'll find out that every single time that we have entered battle, with the oppressor—every single time, one hundred percent—we have won.

—Grassroots Grandmother **Elizabeth Marshall,** Eskasoni First Nation

INTRODUCTION

Since time immemorial, Indigenous societies all over the world have often been thought of as warrior societies. That is because, according to Indigenous belief systems, the warrior must protect not only the birds, animals, plants, fish, and insects, but also the land, water, mountains, rivers, and skies of their traditional territories. You see, Indigenous cultures believe all of life is interconnected. This belief is called **Netukulimk** by the L'nu'k of Mi'kma'ki.

Indigenous warriors are activists and heroes seeking to defend their livelihood, natural habitat, and people.

In this way, we consider every **L'nu** profiled in this book to be a warrior. But some L'nu'k deserve special mention for their work as activists, making the world a better place, and it's those warriors who you'll find in this section.

SMA'KNIS SERGEANT SAM GLOADE
FOUR HUNDRED AND FIFTY

Born: April 20, 1880; Died: October 26, 1957
Bear River First Nation, NS

I'll never forget the first night. I stayed out most of the night watching the flares go up over no man's land, like fireworks and hearing the cannons and bursts of rifle and machine gun fire," wrote **Sma'knis** and World War One veteran Sergeant Sam Gloade of his first night in battle.

The Mi'kmaw soldier from Bear River First Nation was in the infantry, then a tunneller for the Sixth Field Company and Battalion. He prepared tunnels under battlefields in Belgium and dugouts at Vimy Ridge, and when one collapsed on twenty soldiers, he saved their lives. Despite all that, his bravest act came after the war was over. After the armistice, or peace treaty, was signed, Sam was sent to search for mines and demolition charges. This was considered a very dangerous job because these bombs could detonate if they weren't expertly removed. He removed 450 of them.

For all these demonstrations of remarkable courage, Corporal Sam Gloade was awarded the Distinguished Conduct Medal, the British War Medal, and the Victory Medal. He was buried with his three medals when he passed away in 1957.

DID YOU KNOW?

Throughout history, **Sma'knisk** *(warriors) have fought and died for human and treaty rights. Many volunteered to fight and die for Canada and its allies in World Wars One and Two and the Korean War. Many also served as peacekeepers. Once in the trenches, as with other Indigenous soldiers, Sma'knisk were often assigned the most miserable and dangerous tasks—such as sniper duty, reconnaissance scouting, and tunnelling. Yet despite their bravery and sacrifice, these soldiers returned to their home countries to face even more racism. Those returning after World War One were denied the War Veteran's Allowance, for example, while many World War One and World War Two vets lost their "Indian" status because Canada's Indian Act said they could not keep it if they left the reserve for more than four years.*

A problematic legal term, "Indian status" was created by the Canadian government as a way for them to decide who was and who was not "Indian." Having Indian status gives Indigenous people different benefits for things like health care, education, and taxes. But it's also very easy to lose and not every Indigenous person is eligible for it in the first place.

SMA'KNIS SERGEANT WILFRED C. BASQUE
KULAMAN MA WANTA'SIWK: LEST WE FORGET

Born: 1945; Died: 1998
Sipekne'katik First Nation, NS

"**O**ur veterans had a hard time. They weren't even allowed to vote," Rosie Basque told the CBC in 2019. "There was a lot of obstacles they faced."

Basque's husband, Sergeant Wilfred C. Basque, was in the US Marine Corps and fought in the Vietnam War (1955–1975). He was an L'nu from Sipekne'katik First Nation. Rosie recalled how her husband had trouble going to sleep because he was always thinking about his friends, other Sma'knisk.

"He said, 'Oh my God, my mind is going really fast…I'm thinking about Veterans Day," Rosie recalled. "The next morning, when I woke up, he told me, 'Rose, I wrote this poem.'"

After reading "Sma'knis," Rosie suggested Wilfred type it up and make photocopies to give out. After some edits and rewrites, her husband did just that. The poem, chronicling the many sacrifices of Sma'knisk on Canada's behalf, begins as follows:

> I have always kept returning ever since the day I was born
> Each time your drum and circle called, my soul was ripped
>   and torn
> Forever as I picked up my lance, my quiver and my bow
> The eagle soaring me on high would swoop down and drop
>   me low

But it is my duty to fight for my people and for my nation
The test and trials of war are but my sacred tribulations
I am called Sma'knis

The reading of the poem "Sma'knis" by Wilfred C. Basque has become a central part of Indigenous Veterans Day ceremonies and Remembrance Day ceremonies in Mi'kma'ki. Next November 8, Indigenous Veterans Day, be sure to pay tribute to Mi'kmaw soldiers, or Sma'knisk, for their courage and dedication that protected generations to come.

SAQAMAW NOEL JEDDORE
A GOLD MEDAL ON A SAINT

Born: December 18, 1865; Died: May 14, 1944
Miawpukek First Nation, NL

Known as **Saqamaw** (Chief) Noel Jeddore to the English, Saqamaw Noel Geodol was born in the late 1800s in Miawpukek First Nation, nestled in the southern interior of Newfoundland, or "Ktaqmkuk," as it is known in Mi'kmaw. Back then, thousands of woodland caribou roamed the bush and barrens, and the Mi'kmaq had access to a plentiful supply of small game like fox, muskrat, beaver, and fish, while a bounty of gooseberries, blueberries, and strawberries dotted the hillsides and valleys in summer. Since their conversion by a French priest in the 1600s, the Mi'kmaq of Miawpukek were also known as devout Christians—they built their first church in Conne River just a few years after Noel was born.

Everything would change when Father St. Croix was appointed permanent priest for the region in 1916. Settling nearby in St. Alban's where he held church services, the priest soon used his influence to dismantle the language and customs of local Mi'kmaq. Concerned they were mocking God, he forbade the singing of hymns and praying in Mi'kmaw. He also demanded that all Mi'kmaw couples end their courtships unless they were willing to marry, and that all teachers cease using the Mi'kmaw language. Anyone brave enough to defy the Father's wishes was either banned from the church or threatened with damnation.

Three years later, Noel became the Saqamaw of Miawpukek. As Saqamaw, he also became the guardian of a prayer book called *Komqwej wi'kasikl*. Watermarked 1807, the book transcribed the Lord's Prayer and Hail Mary in Mi'kmaw hieroglyphics, and he used it to lead Sunday service in the community. He was also appointed guardian of the gold medal given to his predecessor by the Grand Council. According to oral history passed down by his great-great-grandson, whenever Noel wore his medal to Sunday mass, the people came to him and kissed it.

It was around this time that a rumour began circulating—the church in St. Alban's would be rebuilt in Miawpukek. Given Father St. Croix was based in St. Alban's, he was greatly upset by this rumour, so Noel called a community meeting to discuss the matter. According to historical records, during the meeting Noel remarked that if his community were "forced to abandon their church, faith, and language, they would have murder in their hearts." Learning of the remarks, the Father mistook them as a direct threat to his life, and contacted the local police force, who soon presented Noel with an ultimatum: either go to prison or into exile. Noel decided on the latter, and moved to Eskasoni, Unama'kik. It's said that "many of his people followed him into exile, never to return to their homes."

Before leaving he took the gold medal, draped it over the statue of St. Anne, the Patron Saint of the Mi'kmaq, and said: "I go, but the medal, it stays here now." According to Noel's great-great-grandson, that medal stayed there for a long time; no succeeding Saqamaw would dare wear it. "I believe it was more than just my father that left the community that day," John Nick Jeddore wrote, quoting his grandfather, Noel's son, almost a hundred years later.

The medal was not worn again until 1980, when Grand Chief Donald (Senior) Marshall appointed William Joe as the Traditional Saqamaw: Chief of the Ktaqmkuk Mi'kmaq for life.

After Noel's departure, very few people continued to speak Mi'kmaw in Miawpukek, and this quickly spread throughout Ktaqmkuk as a whole. Only within the past few decades, under the leadership of Saqamaw Mi'sel Joe, has there been a language resurgence, with Mi'kmaw language classes slowly cropping up in First Nations' schools across Ktaqmkuk, like the first crocuses of spring, signalling a long-awaited rebirth.

SAQAMAW
OLIVER LEBOBE
L'NUEY

Born: 1779; Died: 1849
Epekwitk (PEI)

orn 1779, the same year the Mi'kmaq and the British signed the last Peace and Friendship Treaty, Saqamaw Oliver Lebobe was one of the first L'nu'k to officially take a stand for the Mi'kmaq of Epekwitk, also known as Prince Edward Island.

In 1832, Epekwitk L'nu'k were not doing well, with many living in hunger and poverty. Driven to help their people, Oliver and other Epekwitnewaq Chiefs sent a letter to PEI's colonial government, describing their concerns that the Mi'kmaq, with no land on which to grow crops, were faring poorly. And while the PEI government acknowledged the letter, nothing changed over the next several years. Frustrated and determined to help his people, in 1838, Oliver wrote another letter, this time to the Queen of England herself.

In his letter to Queen Victoria, Oliver explicitly pointed out that the British were refusing to honour their Peace and Friendship Treaties. In taking over Mi'kmaw lands, he went on to say, PEI's colonial settlers had taken away any means for his people to provide for themselves, such as hunting and growing food. The Mi'kmaq of PEI, he said, desperately needed somewhere to settle, "on this, our native Island," without fear of mistreatment or being driven off. This letter—from a man truly of the people—finally got the attention of the PEI government.

And while Oliver never lived to see his dream realized—he passed away in 1849 at the age of seventy—the PEI government finally granted local Mi'kmaq their own lands in 1853.

KJI-KEPTIN GABRIEL SYLLIBOY
A TRUE LEADER

Born: August 18, 1874; Died: March 4, 1964
We'koqma'q First Nation, NS

The first ever *elected* **Kji-keptin** (Grand Chief) of the **Sante' Mawio'mi** (the Mi'kmaq Grand Council), Gabriel Sylliboy was a celebrated religious leader his entire life. "When he spoke, you could hear a pin drop. He had a lot of respect from the people," Peter Paul, his grandson, said. Treaty educator Jaime Battiste agreed, claiming that wherever Gabriel walked, out of respect, people stopped and waited until he passed.

Standing up for the rights of his people, Gabriel Sylliboy is believed to be the first Mi'kmaw to defend himself using the land rights he and all L'nu'k were granted through the 1752 Peace and Friendship Treaties. In 1927, Gabriel was arrested under the Lands and Forests Act for hunting muskrat and possessing pelts out of season while off his We'koqma'q reserve. Throughout his subsequent trial, R. v. Sylliboy (1928), Gabriel argued that the 1752 Peace and Friendship Treaty signed between Mi'kmaw Chief Jean Baptiste Cope and the British Crown acknowledged the rights of his people to freely hunt and fish on their unceded (never surrendered) land. "It is agreed that the said Tribe of Indians shall not be hindered from but have free liberty of Hunting & Fishing as usual," states the Treaty. Yet despite the supporting testimony of five other L'nu'k, Gabriel was convicted of all charges.

The Kji-keptin died nearly four decades later in 1964, and twenty-two years after that, the decision in his case was overturned and he was found not guilty.

In 1986, the presiding judge with the Supreme Court of Canada wrote: "The language used in [Kji-keptin Gabriel Sylliboy's] case reflected the biases and prejudices of another era in [Canada's] history. This language is no longer acceptable."

After receiving petitions from Gabriel's family and other L'nu'k, Gabriel was also granted a posthumous (after-death) pardon. On February 16, 2017, both Nova Scotia's Lieutenant Governor and Premier Stephen McNeil formally acknowledged his conviction was in error, while the then premier made a direct, public apology to Gabriel's grandson George Sylliboy.

"Grand Chief Gabriel Sylliboy's efforts were courageous and brave," said then Kji-keptin Ben Sylliboy following the pardon's announcement. "Today the Mi'kmaq celebrate our constitutionally protected aboriginal and treaty rights in large part because of people like him. The free pardon and apology ensure that...despite his conviction, our late Grand Chief was right all along."

Kji-keptin Gabriel Sylliboy's pardon can be found on full display today in the lobby of Nova Scotia's Province House.

ELDER RACHAEL MARY MARSHALL
IT TAKES A COMMUNITY

Born: 1909; Died: 1997
Millbrook First Nation, NS

Throughout her life, Rachael Mary Marshall fought to improve the living conditions of fellow L'nu'k. At the age of nine, young Rachael Mary penned a letter and mailed it to Ottawa. In the letter, she explained a fellow band member was not receiving enough food and demanded the government do something to help. Later becoming one of Canada's first elected female First Nations Chiefs, she seemed to shape her life around the idea that it takes a community to raise a child.

A mother to ten, Rachael Mary served as Millbrook First Nation's Chief from 1969 to 1971. During this time, she approached Jean Chrétien, then minister of Indian Affairs, explaining again that local Mi'kmaq were starving and in need of more assistance. The future prime minister refused to help, but his attempts to silence Rachael Mary only doubled her resolve as an activist for her community.

Crusading on behalf of Indigenous women, especially those who suddenly lost their "Indian status" after marrying a non-Indigenous person, Rachael became an early public supporter of the Nova Scotia Native Women's Association. Founded in 1972, the Nova Scotia Native Women's Association advocates for Indigenous women and their families.

Throughout her golden years, Rachael Mary went on to enjoy several grandchildren. One such grandchild, the renowned artist Alan Syliboy, tried to articulate her powerful presence in words.

"She was a forward thinker," he told *The Xavierian*. "Always open minded. We could talk to her anytime about anything. She was radical in her own way too. She made some people nervous, especially the priests. If she would disapprove of them, she would say something. They all had to pass the test to go see her, of course. They had to go see Rachael Marshall."

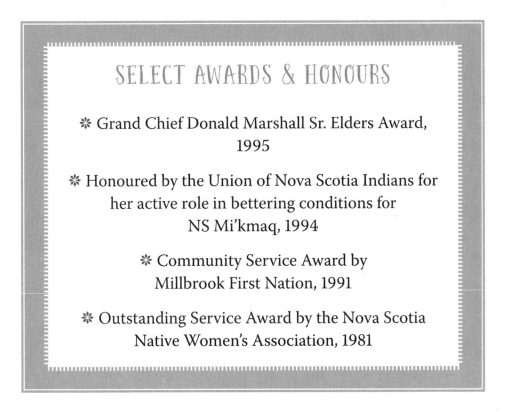

SELECT AWARDS & HONOURS

❇ Grand Chief Donald Marshall Sr. Elders Award,
1995

❇ Honoured by the Union of Nova Scotia Indians for
her active role in bettering conditions for
NS Mi'kmaq, 1994

❇ Community Service Award by
Millbrook First Nation, 1991

❇ Outstanding Service Award by the Nova Scotia
Native Women's Association, 1981

DONALD MARSHALL JR.
ONE MAN'S CONVICTION

Born: September 13, 1952; Died: August 6, 2009
Membertou First Nation, NS

Donald Marshall Jr. was the oldest of Donald and Caroline Marshall's thirteen children. Known as "Junior" to family and close friends, he was eleven when his father, Donald Senior, became the second elected Grand Chief of the Mi'kmaw Nation. A few years later, Junior's rebellious streak kicked in, and, at fifteen, he was expelled from his all-white school for striking a teacher. Just shy of his seventeenth birthday, he was sentenced to four months in county jail after he was caught buying alcohol for other minors.

A few months later he was hanging out at a park and witnessed the murder of another young man. In less than a week he was falsely charged with the murder and, within six months, found guilty by an all-white jury. He spent the next eleven years in prison before finally getting the case reopened. His wrongful murder conviction was the first one ever overturned in the Canadian justice system. Upon his release in 1982, his first request was to visit Peggys Cove, a fishing village near Halifax, to see the ocean.

While he was already a hero to his people, Donald's most important legacy would begin in 1996, when he was caught catching and selling eel out of season without a license. When officials demanded he stop, he called Membertou Chief Terry Paul instead. "I told him to keep fishing," Chief Paul later said. "I felt strongly that he had a right to be there and gain a livelihood."

Picking up where Gabriel Sylliboy, the first elected Grand Chief, left off, Donald spent three long years in court battles until the highest court of Canada once more said he was not guilty.

In 1999 the Supreme Court of Canada was forced to finally uphold the centuries-old treaty between the Mi'kmaq and British Nations. Further, it confirmed the Mi'kmaq and Wolastoqiyik had the right to earn a moderate livelihood from hunting, fishing, and gathering.

Over the years that followed, Donald would struggle to build relationships and a healthy life for himself. Nonetheless he also ran camps for at-risk Indigenous youth until his health deteriorated and he passed in 2009.

"He was not going to be bullied by the justice system into taking the easy way out," Bruce Archibald, a Dalhousie law professor, told the *Toronto Star* after Donald's passing. With regards to the wrongful murder conviction in particular, "He could have gotten out on parole many years earlier if he had been willing to [say] that he did it. And he stood firm on that."

Jim Maloney, the chief investigator in the Royal Commission's wrongful murder conviction, later told *Saltwire News*, "You can't mention treaties without Marshall, freedom without Marshall, justice denied without Marshall. He's our Martin Luther King. Our hero. Our light in the sky."

When asked how he felt about the Supreme Court's ruling to overturn his fishing charges in 1999, the soft-spoken Donald said, "I was there for my people, [so] it was more touching than anything else."

In 2018, the Donald Marshall Junior Centre for Justice and Reconciliation was officially opened in Wagmatcook First Nation, Unama'kik, in his honour. Housing a provincial court as well as the family division of Nova Scotia's Supreme Court, the centre incorporates Indigenous justice traditions and customs including a Healing and Wellness Court. It's the first of its kind in Canada.

RESTORATIVE JUSTICE

Indigenous justice practices focus on healing and accountability (which is when the person who did something wrong accepts blame) rather than punishment. This is usually called "restorative justice" and looks at the reasons why someone might have committed a crime. Unlike a colonial legal process that usually only involves lawyers, judges, and jury members, a restorative justice program involves the whole community. Sometimes sentencing after a crime is delayed for up to two years to allow the offender to work through a personal healing plan first.

ELDER DORENE BERNARD
THE WATER-WALKING GRANDMOTHER

Born: July 19th, 1956
Sipekne'katik, NS

A Mi'kmaw Elder and Water Protector, Dorene Bernard was one of the last children to leave Shubenacadie Residential School in 1967. Her father, the late John Bernard, had been one of the first to attend, way back in 1929. He carried the scars of both the residential school and the Vietnam War, and it fell to Dorene's mother, Nancy Lutz, to be the family's rock. Despite having a strong matriarch, when Dorene left Shubenacadie School just a month shy of her eleventh birthday, she said, "I had a big chip on my shoulder. I was really angry that I was put there. It was buried deep in me."

For years after leaving the school, Dorene stayed angry, but when she was just fifteen, she was inspired to channel it towards social justice. "As a teenager growing up, I would see people come to my house…you know, people like [Mi'kmaw activist] Anna Mae Aquash, she was visiting my family. I [would listen] to what they were doing about Indigenous rights and I wanted to go with them… But they told me I was too young."

She would find her calling later in the field of social work. After starting out in child welfare, Dorene continues to work with residential school survivors to this day. As a mother to

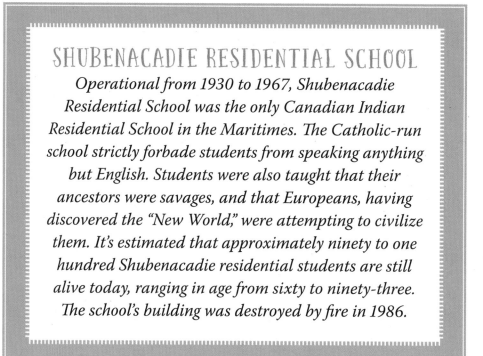

SHUBENACADIE RESIDENTIAL SCHOOL
Operational from 1930 to 1967, Shubenacadie Residential School was the only Canadian Indian Residential School in the Maritimes. The Catholic-run school strictly forbade students from speaking anything but English. Students were also taught that their ancestors were savages, and that Europeans, having discovered the "New World," were attempting to civilize them. It's estimated that approximately ninety to one hundred Shubenacadie residential students are still alive today, ranging in age from sixty to ninety-three. The school's building was destroyed by fire in 1986.

four and grandmother to nine, Dorene founded the Grassroots Grandmothers Circle in 2008 after posing the question: "How can we help our people, our L'nu community?" in a shake tent ceremony. (During a shake tent ceremony, a spiritual leader will invite anyone who wishes to be healed inside a tent to sing, drum, and welcome spirit helpers to answer questions and offer solutions to problems.) The answer Dorene received took the form of a community action collective of women, men, youth, and, yes, grandmothers determined to heal the Mi'kmaw Nation.

As a devoted Water Protector, Dorene said most Canadian communities, unlike many First Nations, have had little to no exposure to water shortage. "Unless you are without your water… you take for granted that there will always be clean tap water," she told the Mi'kma'ki Water Symposium. She explained that the Mi'kmaq view water as sacred. "When we are in the womb, we are in the water. With that gift comes the responsibility to protect the water. When our water is not clean, our plants, our medicines, our food—everything—is affected. We need water for all life," she said. "Water is life."

In 2017, Dorene's success as an activist was formally recognized by the Coady International Institute when she was appointed the first female Indigenous Chair in Social Justice. The following year she also published a journal article called "Reconciliation and Environmental Racism in Mi'kma'ki." Along with her work in academia, Dorene consults with residential school survivors on behalf of the Indian Residential School Survivors Legacy Project. Just days before the first buried remains of residential school children were unearthed in Kamloops, British Columbia, in 2021, she met with Shubenacadie school survivors to designate the former Shubenacadie school grounds a national historic site—the result of a process involving both Canadian and Mi'kmaw national governments.

ELDER LORRAINE WHITMAN
FOR INDIGENOUS WOMEN'S SAKE

Born: June 19, 1960
Glooscap First Nation, NS

orn the same year Canada granted all Indigenous people the right to vote, Elder Lorraine Whitman is one of the fourteen children of Elder Doris (née Brooks) and Chief Joseph Peters. During the 1930s, her grandfather, Louis Peters, was also the Chief of Bear River First Nation. Two of Lorraine's siblings have also gone on to be Chiefs.

"He was such a well-educated man," said Lorraine, recalling her grandfather, who passed away in 1963. "I vaguely remember this great big man [with] a very soft voice, like his voice didn't go with his body. And he'd always say, if we follow the right road, the Red Road, we will be able to open the hearts of many people and move forward."

Adorned with the spirit name "Grandmother White Sea Turtle" by two Mi'kmaw Elders, Lorraine's Red Road forward can be traced back to primary school, when she first stood up to the boy who called her a "stinky, dirty, rotten Indian."

"And with that, I thought, you know, I'm not going to let this happen to anyone else," she said.

True to her word, Lorraine advocates for Indigenous rights on a daily basis. In 2019, after serving as president of the Nova Scotia Native Women's Association, Lorraine became president of the Native Women's Association of Canada (NWAC). In 2020, she contributed an opinion piece to the *Halifax Chronicle Herald*

DID YOU KNOW?

As mentioned earlier, the origin of the name Turtle Island (what many Indigenous people call North America) can be traced back through oral history to the story of a turtle holding the entire world on its back. In many Indigenous cultures, the turtle is also symbolic of an individual, family, or band of the highest rank. According to Mi'kmaw legend, Glooscap's mother is a female turtle. Glooscap is the mythical supernatural Indigenous hero who created Mi'kma'ki.

calling for police reform. She reflected on the recent death of twenty-six-year-old Chantel Moore, a New Brunswick–area Indigenous woman "armed with nothing but a knife" who was killed by police.

Lorraine said she feels the recent unearthing of Indigenous children's remains on residential school sites might convince both First Nations and Canada to work together.

"We've always known that, but now that Canada's aware, we need to work together and we need to forgive. And you know, that's one of the hardest things, to forgive when your loved ones have been murdered or killed. There's a dark cloud hanging over us. But we need to remove that dark cloud and we need to work together."

In her personal time, Lorraine mentors Indigenous children and finds new ways to bring Indigenous culture and heritage to the forefront in Canada. For example, in 2017, she developed the Seven Sacred Teachings Coffee for Just Us! Coffee, with a portion

DID YOU KNOW?

According to the Mi'kmaw tradition, the Seven Sacred Teachings—Love, Honesty, Humility, Respect, Truth, Patience, and Wisdom—assign spiritual awareness and moral respect to all living things. The Mi'kmaq believe that anyone who lives according to these Seven Sacred Teachings will also undergo some type of transformation every seven years.

of the fair-trade coffee proceeds directed towards select Indigenous programs. "The passion for the Indigenous people is where I follow my heart," she explained.

SELECT AWARDS & HONOURS

❋ Queen's Jubilee Platinum Award, 2022

❋ Honorary Doctorate of Humanities,
Acadia University, 2022

❋ Mi'kmaq Language Advisory representative, 2020

❋ Grand Chief Donald Marshall Sr. Elders Award,
2020

❋ Member of the Mi'kmawey Debert Elders
Advisory Council

❋ Nova Scotia Volunteer Award, 2019

❋ President of the Native Women's Association of
Canada (NWAC), 2019 to 2022

❋ Elder for Acadia University, 2018 to present

DR. PAMELA PALMATER
WARRIOR WOMAN

Ugpi'Ganjig First Nation, NB

"Everybody has a different concept of what a hero is," said Pam Palmater. "To me, heroes are warriors. Warriors who continue to fight and push forward—despite the racism, genocide, colonization, discrimination—every barrier that's been put in front of our people, they continue to fight and fight and just push forward."

For as long as she can remember, Pam's family has taught her to push for the rights of Mi'kmaw and Wolastoqiyik Nations. "Family is our first source of a traditional Mi'kmaw education. They teach us what our history is, what we're fighting for, how to nation-build, and how to assert our rights. Family is everything to me."

From a family of eight sisters and three brothers, Pam said her father, Frank Palmater Senior, was a natural-born warrior, through and through. Along with being a World War Two veteran, Pam said Sma'knis Frank Palmater also fought racism his entire life.

"My dad will always be a hero to me," she said. "One of the things I remember most about him is every time I saw him, he had a new book for me. It could have been one he bought at a church basement sale or borrowed from a library, but he always had books...Because he wanted me to never accept what I'm told and to learn...[to] look at life critically and reflect on what I'm seeing. Never stop trying to know, be, and do better."

Once described by the YWCA as "a trailblazing model for young Indigenous women, planting seeds of change that are transforming Indigenous communities across Canada," Pam has never stopped fighting and pushing for better. In fact, it's hardly a stretch to describe this world-renowned lawyer, professor, and media commentator—not to mention host of *The Warrior Life Podcast* and *Warrior Kids Podcast*—as a warrior herself.

Pam was one of the spokespeople and educators of Idle No More in 2012, helping lead the social movement resisting Canada's racist laws. She also demanded better in 2020, stepping up for the Mi'kmaq after non-Indigenous people protested the Mi'kmaw treaty right to fish under their own laws. Non-Indigenous fishers claimed that Mi'kmaw fishers were taking too many fish, and they turned to racially provoked violence and vandalism to scare the Mi'kmaw fishers away. Frustrated because Canada wouldn't step in and protect these L'nu'k, Pam—with the support of Sipekne'katik First Nation Chief Mike Sack, two other Mi'kmaw lawyers,

SELECT AWARDS & HONOURS

❋ Knowledge Mobilization Award, Institute for Research on Public Policy, 2022

❋ Toronto's Most Inspiring Women, *Streets of Toronto*, 2021

❋ 100 Most Influential People in 2021 in Government & Politics, *The Hill Times*, 2021

❋ Power List: Top 25 Most Influential Movers & Shakers, *Financial Post Magazine*, 2017

❋ Award for Excellence in Human Rights, Atlantic Human Rights Centre, 2017

❋ Top 25 Most Influential Lawyers: Top 5 in Human Rights, *Canadian Lawyer Magazine*, 2013

and the human rights group "Justice for Girls"—called on the United Nation's Committee on the Elimination of Racial Discrimination (CERD) to protect the Mi'kmaw fishers.

"It is shameful that we had to seek international intervention, but Canada's racist laws, policies, and practices continue to breach our basic human rights and inherent Mi'kmaw rights to our lands, waters, and fishery," she told the CBC. The United Nations responded, calling on Canada to put a stop to the racist violence against Mi'kmaw fishers. "[We] hope this will be a wakeup call for Canada," she said.

And while Pam stands united with a legion of Indigenous warriors ready to protect Mi'kma'ki and the rest of Turtle Island, she said this sort of hard work is ultimately everyone's responsibility. "It is vital that we protect our culture and identity, for our heirs and their heirs forever." And she wants every little L'nu to know they're protected too.

"Even if bad things are happening, remember how important you are. We're always connected to all of these radiating circles of extended families on and off reserve, within our territory. Know you are backed up by Mi'kmaw warriors working hard to bring everybody back home into our Nation," she said. "We will be here when you're ready."

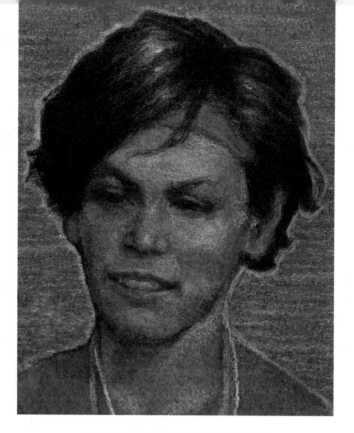

LANDYN TONEY
LIGHTING THE TORCH

Born: July 2, 2008
Annapolis Valley First Nation, NS

efore the terrible discovery of Indigenous children's unmarked graves in Kamloops, BC, Landyn Toney was just another twelve-year-old kid enjoying summer break. Back then, he said, he knew almost nothing about residential schools. And what he learned made him angry.

"When I heard about all the numbers going up for the graves that they found for the residential schools, that just made me mad,"

Landyn said. "I wanted to show my anger by doing something good."

Determined to help, Landyn shared an idea with his mom. She was immediately on board. Within a few days, the pair mapped out "Landyn's Journey of Awareness"—a 203-kilometre walk designed to draw attention to the trauma suffered by Indigenous children at residential schools. Starting off from their home in Bible Hill, NS, they chose to end their walk in Annapolis Valley First Nation, Landyn's birthplace—a decision made to intentionally highlight how many residential school children never made it back home to their reserve.

Setting off on Canada Day 2021, thousands joined them along the way to show their support. "Usually teachers are the adults," a retired schoolteacher told APTN. "This time Landyn is the teacher."

Even Prime Minister Justin Trudeau sent along encouragement via Twitter: "Know that you're making a difference—and people across the country are with you, every step of the way."

Six days later, when Landyn and his mom finally set foot on the streets of Annapolis Valley First Nation, the community gave them a heroes' welcome.

And while both admit they still feel a little overwhelmed by all the attention, they said they hope to keep the campaign going with a Canada-wide torch relay some day in the future.

"So the plan is to organize walks in different reserves across Canada, then walk so far and pass the torch on to someone else," Landyn's mom said. While happy to pass the torch, Landyn agreed that walks like theirs are a small sacrifice to pay compared to what residential school survivors experienced.

"Because the survivors, they had to go through all that, and they had to see their brothers and sisters die in front of them," he said.

Until they pass the torch on to the next heroes, Landyn said both he and his mom are happy to have shone a light on the issues faced by so many Indigenous people. "It was all worth it."

PART II

ARTISTS

❝I want to be a positive role model for other Indigenous people—that's the lane I'm choosing to do this in. I want to be the bright light in a sea of darkness.❞

–Indigenous Rap Artist **Tristan Grant (Wolf Castle)**,
Pabineau First Nation

❝I wish more of my people would write the beautiful stories I hear them tell.❞

–Poet Laureate of the Mi'kmaq, **Rita Joe**,
We'koqma'q First Nation

❝The fashion world, the music world, the film world—Indigenous people should and need to be there. And that's something we want the youth to understand. That essentially being yourself and representing your culture can take you really far.❞

–Bead Artist & Entrepreneur **Cheyenne Isaac-Gloade**,
Listuguj First Nation

RILEY BERNARD
MI'KMAW SUPERHEROES

Born: August 1993
Epekwitk (PEI)

When COVID-19 hit in the winter of 2020, Riley Bernard was hanging out with an Elder of Abegweit First Nation in Scotchfort. They talked about how much the world was changing.

"More of the old ways are going to come back," the Elder said.

Researching Mi'kmaw legends and turning them into the graphic novel *Kinap Legends* is Riley's way of sharing his love of his people's stories with today's generation.

"Since I was a kid, I was really into Spider-Man and the Teenage Mutant Ninja Turtles. I think I just loved movies in general and I wanted to tell stories," Riley said. Riley bought his first comic book, *Hawkeye*, when he was ten years old.

His second graphic novel, *Kinap Legends*, is told through the perspective of a thriving and adventurous Mi'kmaw in pre-contact Mi'kma'ki. It relates stories of the family's encounters with Saqamaws (Chiefs) and **Keptins** (Captains) in Mi'kmaw villages, some of which have superpowers, Riley said.

"They have this ability to harness power from both within them or outside of them…power to make themselves invulnerable to damage, super strong, some of them can even go invisible," he said.

The first seeds of *Kinap Legends* came from his former manager, Ron Zakar, with Mi'kmaq Heritage Actors, a PEI theatre troupe.

Riley was twenty-two and performing with the group when Zakar said he thought a graphic novel about the legends would be cool.

"Ron likes grabbing hold of artists and squeezing art out of them," said Riley. "He bought me poster boards and wanted me to make big charcoal sketches of the Mi'kmaw legends. So I actually did it."

But before beginning *Kinap Legends*, he first wanted to finish *The Stick Persons* comic series, an idea he'd had since high school. Only after *The Stick Persons* was published in 2019 did he remember to go back to his former manager's idea. Then he decided to start looking deeper into Mi'kmaw history.

After reading *Legends of the Micmacs*, a nineteenth-century book written by Canadian missionary Silas Rand, he knew he was onto something big. He remembers thinking: "This is so interesting and fascinating. This has to be a comic book."

Riley went on to explain: "Back then [Rand] went around to communities to get their stories and write them down…some [were] Mi'kmaw women and Elders around Charlottetown and Rocky Point. So, I use a lot of that for inspiration."

Riley said he feels storytelling and language-keeping are crucial to keeping cultures alive, and he's worried some Mi'kmaw stories could get lost. "While I grew up with my grandparents, I never noticed how lucky I was to be with them, listening to them speak Mi'kmaw together."

In 2021 he applied for and received a $1,000 grant from a provincial program to support Indigenous artists.

"I just want to make a good story about some relatable characters and Mi'kmaw history. That seems to be my ultimate goal. Just to get people to learn more."

And while Riley and his life and business partner, Jessica Francis, are working on the second edition of *Kinap Legends*, they're also busy teaching their two-year-old daughter Mi'kmaw.

"She's at a perfect age, like a sponge, learning how to communicate. Her brain is on rapid fire. We make sure to say Mi'kmaw words like 'Good morning,' and 'Come here,' and 'Do you want water?' Stuff like that. So yeah, we're just getting started."

Kinap Legends and *The Stick Persons* are both published by Shoot from the Hip Comics, an independent comic book publisher in Charlottetown, PEI.

ELDER RITA JOE
GENTLE WARRIOR POET

Born: March 15, 1932; Died: March 20, 2007
We'koqma'q First Nation, NS

Future poet laureate of the Mi'kmaq, Rita (née Bernard) Joe rose from humble beginnings. Born during the Great Depression, she was the youngest of Joseph and Annie (née Googoo) Bernard's seven children, and only five years old when her mother died during childbirth. Her father sent her to live in a foster home, only to leave for the Spirit World himself five years later. Officially orphaned at ten, Rita had cycled through a series of homes by the time she wrote to the Indian Agent at age twelve, requesting admission to the Indian Residential School in Shubenacadie, Nova Scotia. Indian Agents were officials working on First Nation reserves on behalf of the Canadian government. "Please come and get me on Wednesday," she wrote, later admitting she was anxious about a toxic home environment.

Rita remained at Shubenacadie until 1948, when at the age of sixteen, she packed up one change of clothes and headed to Halifax. She earned her first paycheque working twelve-hour shifts at the Halifax Infirmary, setting aside a portion to buy a pair of red shoes. A single mother a year later, she gave her first child to her sister. When she became pregnant shortly thereafter, she left for Boston in search of work. There she met Frank Joe, a member of Eskasoni First Nation, and the two married in 1959. According to Rita, her husband often remarked, "You are a witch, but a good witch."

The two returned to Eskasoni to raise a family. She published her poems in Eskasoni's *MicMac News* in 1968, where she was soon granted her own column called "Here and There in Eskasoni."

Rita's fate was sealed the day her second oldest, Evelyn, asked permission to drop out of school. It was 1971. That morning Evelyn's Grade 11 teacher had directed her to stand before the class and explain why her ancestors behaved like the savages depicted in their history text. Evelyn refused.

"What's portrayed in the history books is not the truth," Rita told her daughter. And with that, Rita's war had begun, and it was waged gently, with words.

Rita referred to herself as "a housewife with a dream." Her vision was to bring laughter "to the sad eyes of my people," and her writing developed in earnest. Her first collection, *Poems of Rita Joe*, was published in 1978 to critical acclaim.

She would go on to publish six more books and mentor young writers, championing Mi'kmaw culture at every turn. In the early 1990s she used her jackpot winnings from a local bingo to purchase a small building and move it to her Eskasoni property. She named it **Minuitaqn** (Recreate) and became an entrepreneur. "It was an instant success," she said, "because so many people in the community are creative." This became a craft shop as well as her office outside the home for writing.

Another of Rita's daughters once asked her how she came to write her poems. "The words are floating through the air, and I just catch them," Rita replied. And while the world-renowned poet started to run in some pretty distinguished circles (she met Queen Elizabeth II in 1992), her dedication to her craft and her people never faded.

"In 1948, when I was sixteen, the train I entered at Shubenacadie station started to move away from the station. I looked up to the hill, leaving the home I depended on when I was twelve years old… [and] giggled to my heart's content upon leaving the place. 'I'm on my own,' I thought. Wake up when I want, eat as much as I want, dress any way I want. Speak Mi'kmaw until I'm satisfied."

When she passed away in 2007 at the age of seventy-five, a half-finished poem was still in her typewriter.

SELECT AWARDS, HONOURS & PUBLICATIONS

❋ *We are the Dreamers: Recent and Early Poetry,* 1999; *Song of Rita Joe: Autobiography of a Mi'kmaq Poet, 1996; Lnu and Indians We're Called, 1991; Song of Eskasoni: More Poems of Rita Joe, 1988; Poems of Rita Joe, 1978*

❋ Contributing author, *The Mi'kmaq Anthology,* 1997; *Kelusultiek: Original Women's Voices of Atlantic Canada,* 1994

❋ Honorary Doctorate of Letters, Mount Saint Vincent University, 1998, and University College of Cape Breton, 1997

❋ National Aboriginal Achievement Award (now *Indispire*), 1997

❋ Honorary Doctorate of Laws, Dalhousie University, 1993

❋ Member of the Queen's Privy Council, 1992

❋ Member of the Order of Canada, 1989

TRISTAN GRANT
YOUNG, INDIGENOUS, AND PROUD OF IT

Born: 1996
Pabineau First Nation, NB

For as long as he can remember, Tristan Grant has dreamed of becoming a successful rapper.

"I wanted to be a performer and a rapper so bad that sometimes I couldn't sleep at night," Tristan said. "I just had this big dream in my head."

While Tristan was bullied at school "for being poor and Native," he said, he was also surrounded by dreamers and doers. Growing up on the rez, his grandparents' place was "like a second home,"

just two doors down. His granddad, Elder Gilbert Sewell—
a renowned Mi'kmaw artist, Knowledge Keeper, and historian—
often captivated young Tristan with his storytelling skills. A
celebrated filmmaker, his mother, Phyllis Grant, released her own
album in 2008 under the name MO3. And his uncle, the Canadian
rap artist Red Suga, became a household name in the early 2000s.
Tristan vividly recalled his perspective as a boy, watching his mom
and uncle perform live at the 2003 Indigenous Music Awards. "It
was mind-blowing, to see how far that sort of passion and drive
could get you," he said. "From the rez to the Skydome. I think that's
stuck with me from six years old all the way to now."

These influences helped bolster Tristan, who taught himself to play
the piano by age eleven. But it wasn't until his last high school year
that he felt enough confidence to perform in front of a live audience.

"I remember pacing backstage, feeling really scared, and then
thinking, 'I'm going away to university soon, so who cares?' So, we
go out and start the song…and the whole audience just went wild…
I even forgot some of my lyrics [but] nobody cared. I powered
through. And I've just been chasing that ever since."

Despite having no formal musical training, Tristan, now twenty-
seven, has released at least one musical project a year—most
entirely written, recorded, and produced by him—since age
seventeen. Going by the stage name "Wolf Castle," Tristan's already
played at dozens of high-profile festivals, and he's been nominated
for six East Coast Music Awards. With Tupac, Mac Miller, The
Notorious B.I.G., and Tyler, the Creator as some of his influences,
Tristan boldly takes on topics like racism, rebellion, freedom,
and love, all in an attempt to share what it means to be "young,
Indigenous, and proud of it."

"I'm in this oppressed group. I have to deal with this racism all the time, and intergenerational trauma," he told *Next Magazine*. For Tristan, one way to deal with racism is to artfully flip it on its head. Which is probably why the entire video for his single "Get Lit" was shot in a castle, a symbol of British colonialism.

Tristan is determined to make it big—both for himself and for the many Indigenous youth and artists he hopes benefit from his encouragement.

"Art saved my life. It's helped me get out of a lot of negative spaces, and that's the power of it," said Tristan. "Any success I get from this point on, I want to bring as many people as I can along with me."

SELECT AWARDS & HONOURS

❊ Founder, the Emerging Indigenous Artist Grant, Music New Brunswick, 2022

❊ Indigenous Artist of the Year, The Prix Awards, Music New Brunswick (MNB), 2022

❊ Recording of the Year, The Prix Awards, MNB, 2022

❊ Singles and EPs: "Gold Rush", 2020. "Gunna," "Welfman," "Summertime Crush," 2021

❊ Albums: *The Artificial to Original*, 2017; *Rezurbia*, 2018; *DaVinci's Inquest*, 2021

LORETTA GOULD
SHARING HER TEACHINGS

Born: 1976
We'koqma'q First Nation, NS

Renowned quilter and painter Loretta Gould said she owes much to her late mother, Katie Ann Googoo, a seamstress and an extremely proud Mi'kmaw woman.

"The way we were raised, Mom wouldn't let us speak English at all in the house. I despised her for it at the time, but as I got older though I realized I wouldn't be who I am without her."

Inheriting her mother's sewing machine after she passed away, Loretta began sewing quilts after spotting a quilt she couldn't afford in the mall. She soon developed a business of her own, but after fifteen years grew bored of the standard design. So, she decided to try her hand at art quilts.

"I didn't know what I was doing at the time, but I watched some videos, bought some books, and just generally admired other peoples' [art quilts]," she said. "Gradually, though, it just became so natural to me, with the bright colours and so on."

Loretta successfully crafted and sold hundreds of homemade art quilts for another four years, but by 2013, her mother's sewing machine had finally bitten the dust. While Loretta was waiting on repairs, Loretta's oldest, who'd recently taken up painting, asked her mother to join her. Loretta did, and a new passion bloomed. After giving her first acrylic, an owl, to her father, she decided it was time to redirect her talents to painting full time.

Today, Loretta's brightly coloured paintings are sold and exhibited worldwide, conveying vibrant themes of family, nature, and Indigenous culture. She said her greatest honour as an artist so far was in 2016, when she was asked to create and present a commissioned original to Gord Downie, lead singer of The Tragically Hip, who died a year later. The painting, entitled *Share our Teachings*, depicts Downie meeting a young Chanie Wenjack, the subject of one of his last albums, *Secret Path*, surrounded by the Seven Sacred Teachings in animal form.

Loretta said her husband, Elliot, cradled their nine-month-old daughter as they discussed everything from residential schools to family with Gord.

"A very humble man," Loretta said.

Share our Teachings was the first piece Loretta ever created to feature a non-Indigenous person. She's never done so before, or since.

Meanwhile Loretta published her first book, *Counting in Mi'kmaw/Mawkiljemk Mi'kmawiktuk*—illustrated and authored entirely by her—in 2018. And when stores, craft fairs, and galleries shut down during the COVID-19 pandemic, she reinvented herself again—this time expanding into e-commerce. Launched in 2022, her online store features everything from original art prints to designs on greeting cards, stickers, tote bags, and even hooded blankets. To check out Loretta's colourful, Mi'kmaw-inspired merch, visit mikmaq-artist.com.

ELDER GEORGE PAUL
AN HONOURABLE MAN
Metepenagiag First Nation, NB

Born and raised along the Miramichi River in a community called Metepenagiag (Red Bank), Elder George Paul attended the Shubenacadie Residential School from 1960 to 1966. Longing to reconnect with his Mi'kmaw identity, he went on a spiritual quest during the late 1970s and early 1980s. That quest brought him to a series of powwows and sweat lodges across Canada, deep into the woods for days-long fasts, and eventually, back to Metepenagiag.

"You're doing that to show and prove to the spirits that you are sincere," George, whose spirit name is Sky Blue Eagle, said. "That you are willing to go that far to get an understanding."

And while his quest would help him convene with his ancestors' spirits, it would also lead him to discover a deep well of sadness, a place he recognized as part of the collective grief experienced by all of his Mi'kmaw brothers and sisters. As a result, he decided to do whatever was within his power to bring respect and honour back to the Mi'kmaw people. He realized how, after a sweat lodge session with an Elder. The Elder said to George, "You have a song to sing."

A musician his entire adult life, George went home and wrote that song.

Described as haunting—echoing the years of loss and trauma endured by the Mi'kmaq—while also hopeful, healing, and empowering, "The Mi'kmaq Honour Song" was first recorded in

1991, and it has become a sort of anthem for the Mi'kmaq since. Usually performed with drums, it has been played at countless powwows and just about every type of Indigenous gathering since—many of which George helped to coordinate.

"We kind of motivated a trend," he said, noting that powwows are now annual events on the East Coast. George has also given the Wolastoqiyik and the Cree permission to translate the song into their own languages.

George even recorded the song with Symphony Nova Scotia, and recently signed an agreement allowing world-renowned cellist Yo-Yo Ma and Indigenous vocalist Jeremy Dutcher to feature the song on an upcoming album. While it was the first time George had heard of Ma, he soon got up to speed. "Yo-Yo Ma, I mean, that

SELECT AWARDS, HONOURS & PUBLICATIONS

❋ *The Mi'kmaq Honour Song* (children's book), 2019

❋ George Paul and the Red Ochre Band, Best Indigenous Artist/Group of the Year, ECMA 2001

❋ George Paul's original Mi'kmaw chants are sampled in Walt Disney's *Squanto: A Warrior's Tale*, released in 1994 takes it to another level," he said in an interview with Radio Canada.

George and many L'nu'k feel the song has a spirit to it. Some find listening to it helps them abstain from self-destructive behaviors, like addictions, while a young mother said it helped her eight-year-old epileptic boy sleep through the night.

And while he said he dreams of seeing more Indigenous music popularized on mainstream radio, film, and television, George can still be found spreading his love of Mi'kmaw music, spiritual teachings, and people across Mi'kma'ki.

MI'KMAQ HONOUR SONG LYRICS

Roughly translated into English, here are the lyrics in English and Mi'kmaw, with pronunciations too. The first line of each paragraph contains the original Mi'kmaw lyrics. The second, the phonetic pronunciation of these words for English speakers. Finally, the third contains the lyrics translated into English.

Like many songs, "The Mi'kmaq Honour Song" contains a special chant. The chant, "way oh hay hi yah," represents George Paul crying for the loss of his Mi'kmaw culture and way of life. George said he used the chant to help express and process sadness. "There's a spirit that travels with the song," he said.

THE MI'KMAQ HONOUR SONG

Kepmite'tmnej Tan'teli l'nuwulti'kw
Geb-mee-day-d'm'nedge Dawn deli ul'new-ul-dee-k
Let us greatly respect our nativeness

Nikma'jtut Mawita'nej
Neeg-mahj-dewt Ma-wee-dah-nedge
My people let us gather

Kepmite'tmnej Ta'n wettapeksulti'k
Geb-mee-day-d'm'nej Dawn wetta-beg-sul-deeg
Let us greatly respect our aboriginal roots

Nikma'jtut Apoqnmatultinej
Neeg-mahj-dewt Abohn-maw-dul-din-edge
My people, let us help one another

(Hey) Apoqnmatultinej ta'n Kisu'lkw teli ika'luksi'kw
(Hey) abohn-maw-dul-din-edge dawn Gee-suelk deli
   ee-gah-lug-seek
Let us help one another, according to the Creator's

Wla wskitqamu Eye eya
Wulla wuk-seed-hah-moo Way-ah heyo
Intention for putting us on this planet

(The chants below are repeated several times)

Way oh hay hi ya
Ya way yo hay yo hay hi ya
Way yo hay hi ya
Ya way yo hay hi ya
Way yo hay hi ya
Way yo hay hi ya
Ya way yo hay ha ya hay yo

ELDER ALAN SYLIBOY
THE THUNDEROUS MIMIKEJ

Born: September 8, 1952
Millbrook First Nation, NS

While Mi'kmaw is his first language, Alan Syliboy, like so many others, was strictly forbidden from speaking it at school. As a result, he became an increasingly withdrawn student, failing to learn even basic grammar or arithmetic. This, he said, led the nuns to single him out constantly, and eventually assume he wasn't smart enough for school. By the time he'd reached Grade 7, he'd been held back a year three times.

"I excelled at making images under the table in whatever way I could," he said. "My art was sort of an underground movement."

Despite being miserable at school, Alan has fond memories of summer vacations with family and other L'nu'k. "As a child, I spent some time with my stepfather in Pictou, right on the water, and the kids there spoke only Mi'kmaw." The late Rachael Mary Marshall, his grandmother, was also an early supporter. In 1971, she introduced him to Shirley Bear, the accomplished Tobique First Nation artist and activist. Shirley soon took the young prodigy under her wing, helping him set up in Salem, New Hampshire, where Alan soaked up the brave new art world like a sponge.

Alan also credits Shirley with introducing him to petroglyphs, a type of prehistoric art etched in stone. "That changed everything for me because the petroglyphs are central to our history and identity. They helped to answer the question of what makes us unique.

My interest in cultural studies began then and I have basically spent my whole life researching petroglyphs."

Four years later Alan enrolled at the Nova Scotia College of Art and Design (NSCAD), where he interviewed fellow students from as far away as Africa and Europe. "I learned how important it is to research culture. It inspired me to work harder."

After art school, he found work as an oil-burner mechanic, married, and settled down to start a family. After the marriage dissolved, he raised their three children on his own, and opened a studio in Truro. He's worked full time as an artist ever since.

In 1999, Alan created a limited-edition commemorative gold coin for the Canadian Mint. The first ever created by a Mi'kmaw, his coin featured a butterfly, a **mimikej**. Selling all 25,000 copies of the $200 coin, Alan officially shed his figurative cocoon.

Today Alan's signature style—featuring layered petroglyphs and mark-making accented by rich, vibrant colours—is coveted by museum curators and collectors around the world. Showcased alongside famous artists like Salvador Dalí, his mixed-media acrylic paintings soon branched into National Film Board (NFB) animations, public art installations, bestselling books, and award-winning music compilations.

In 2009 Alan teamed up with NFB's Nance Ackerman to launch the short animation *Little Thunder*. In 2013, standing for three consecutive days on scaffolding two storeys high, Alan painted *3D Butterfly*, a five-by-five-metre mural in the main lobby of the Halifax Stanfield International Airport. One of Alan's children's books, *The Thundermaker*, has remained one of Nimbus Publishing's top-selling children's books since its release in 2015. Finally, he is the lead singer of Alan Syliboy and the Thundermakers, his ECMA-nominated band known for musical as well as spoken word, line art, and projected-animation performances.

And that's just to name a few of his creative projects. Much like the petroglyphs he's admired for the past four decades, Alan's Mi'kmaw influences remain deeply etched and enduring in his day-to-day life.

To this day, Alan Syliboy, the world-renowned artist, resides just 250 feet away from his birth home in Millbrook First Nation.

SELECT AWARDS, HONOURS & PUBLICATIONS

❋ Author and illustrator, *Wolverine and Little Thunder*, 2019, and *The Thundermaker*, 2018

❋ Shortlisted for the Masterworks Arts Award for *The Thundermaker*, 2013, and *People of the Dawn*, 2010

❋ Portrait of Grand Chief Membertou, Queen Elizabeth II Commission, Royal Canadian Tour, 2010

❋ Featured Animation, *Little Thunder*, Vancouver Olympics, 2010

❋ Illustrator, *The Stone Canoe: Two Lost Mi'kmaq Tales*, 2007

❋ The Queen's Golden Jubilee Medal, 2002

REBECCA THOMAS
GIRL MAGIC

Born: February 14, 1986
Lennox Island First Nation, PEI

The daughter of Dr. Patricia (née McLean) Thomas and residential school survivor Tim "Redfeather" Thomas, Rebecca Thomas said her parents' marriage ended when she was still a girl. And while her mother packed up Rebecca and her siblings and headed for Riverview, New Brunswick, where Rebecca ultimately grew up, her father, Redfeather, remained a fixture in her and her siblings' lives. Keen to nurture the same pride that the Shubenacadie Residential School attempted to destroy in him, Redfeather often gifted emblems of Indigenous identity—dreamcatchers, beadwork, and animal hides—to his children.

"As a child I believed that I could do and achieve anything," Rebecca said. This feistiness—which she describes in her poem "Ribbons" as magic—combined with her renowned quick wit inspired her dad to nickname her "Swift Fox" as a child.

Yet it wasn't until Rebecca enrolled at Dalhousie University that she decided to explore her Mi'kmaw heritage in earnest.

"The more I learned, the more I got enraged. What was taken from my dad was also taken from me." Yet the more she learned, the more powerful her Indigenous voice became, and slowly her magic resurfaced. In 2013, after watching then Halifax Poet Laureate El Jones perform spoken word, Rebecca became inspired. "I was like, 'I want to do that!'" Shortly after becoming an informal mentor to

SELECT AWARDS, HONOURS & PUBLICATIONS

❊ *I Place You Into the Fire:* Best Canadian Poetry, CBC, 2020

❊ *Swift Fox All Along*: Governor General's Literary Award nomination, 2020

❊ *I'm Finding My Talk*: First Nations Community Read, nominated, 2020; Top 100 Pick, *Globe & Mail*, 2019; CBC Best Picture Book, 2019; Best Atlantic-Published Book Award nominee, 2019; Ann Connor Brimer Award for Children's Literature nominee, 2019; White Ravens selection, 2019.

❊ Halifax Regional Municipality Poet Laureate, 2016–2018

Rebecca, El Jones was performing at an open mic in Halifax and invited her mentee to take the stage. El also recommended Rebecca succeed her as the city's next poet laureate.

"Rebecca's voice fit in that (poet laureate) tradition in terms of someone who would get up and speak about what they knew to be true...without worrying what the response would be," El told the Canadian Press.

In 2016, right on the heels of El Jones, Rebecca became Halifax's first ever Indigenous poet laureate. She's used her public persona to bring Indigenous issues to light ever since.

"I often call on people to be better and become active in making our community a better place. I want people to think for a moment that their perspective as a non-Indigenous person isn't the only perspective," she said. "I don't mince words."

Since finishing her term as poet laureate, Rebecca has continued to write poetry, commentary, and even three books, two of which are for children—*I'm Finding My Talk*, a response poem to Rita Joe's "I Lost My Talk," and *Swift Fox All Along*, a story that uses her own childhood to explore Indigenous identity.

Rebecca said she's often discovered her most authentic voice, or *magic*, by allowing her vulnerability to surface.

"Softness is often seen as passive or ineffective, but I think it has a real power. It takes incredible strength to maintain softness," Rebecca said. "But, if you need to be hard to protect yourself, that's okay, too."

PART III

ATHLETES

> **❝** *The role sport plays in our communities, it's just invaluable. It gives kids a sense of belonging, gives them a sense of friendship. Sports in my culture are second to none.* **❞**

–Chef de Mission, North American Indigenous Games 2023,
Levi Denny, Eskasoni First Nation

> **❝** *I believe that any Indigenous person can make it to the most elite level of whatever area they choose. And you know all it takes? It just takes the right person to guide you.* **❞**

–Former NHL player **Everett Sanipass**, Elsipogtog First Nation

DID YOU KNOW?

The origins of one of Canada's favourite games can be traced way back to before the Europeans arrived, right here in Mi'kma'ki. Master carvers, the Mi'kmaw invented the ice hockey stick. By the turn of the twentieth century, carving hockey sticks was the primary occupation of L'nu'k living in Nova Scotia.

The Starr Manufacturing Company, based out of Dartmouth, NS, sold these "Mic-Mac Hockey Sticks" as early as 1860. In 2006, one of these hand-carved "Mic-Mac Hockey Sticks" was appraised at over six million dollars Canadian.

And while patents didn't exist back then, evidence of the game itself originating here, through the Mi'kmaq, can be found in the language and stories passed down through generations. In 1913, Mi'kmaw ethnographer Dr. Jerry Lonecloud captured the rules for the popular L'nu'k ice sport **duwaken,** *or* **"tu'aqn"** *in the Smith/Francis spelling. As Lonecloud wrote, a "stone carrier" was required to chase "a round stone ball" on the ice with a stick. The stone carrier's job was to "guide the ball away from the other team." The other team's job, in turn, was to "interfere and retrieve it."*

Learn more by watching The Game of Hockey: A Mi'kmaq Story, *a documentary by Cheryl Maloney and her family from Sipekne'katik First Nation, NS.*

LEVI DENNY
CHEF DE MISSION

Born: March 25, 1972
Eskasoni First Nation, NS

"It's going to be huge," Levi Denny said. "It will be the biggest games Nova Scotia has ever hosted. There's probably over five thousand athletes coming."

As Chef de Mission of the 2023 North American Indigenous Games (NAIG), Levi Denny has his work cut out for him. The 2023 games mark the first time Mi'kma'ki has ever hosted the prestigious Indigenous sporting event. Luckily, this Chef has been preparing a long time.

CHEF DE MISSION

Translated from French, the title Chef de Mission *means "head of mission." In the context of sports, it usually refers to the person who leads a national delegation—including athletes, coaches, and other behind-the-scenes team members. One of the primary responsibilities of the Chef de Mission at the North American Indigenous Games (NAIG) is to be the spokesperson for the entire team—both in the lead up to and during the actual games.*

Levi's earliest memory of sport is his earliest memory of life.

"We had a little area to skate in front of our house. I remember being able to walk and then being able to skate," he said.

Raised by his parents, Leonard and Marion Denny, on Eskasoni First Nation, Levi said his home was a hub of proud Mi'kmaw sports enthusiasts. According to Levi, while community leaders ensured youth had access to the local gym and ball fields year-round, his parents also made sure he was enrolled in multiple sports every year, pre-season.

"I'm pretty sure everything we got from Santa Claus growing up was sports-related."

While his first job began as a video lottery technician for his band council, it gradually evolved into full-time sports and recreation work.

"I'm appreciative of the leadership at the time. They realized what a positive impact sports and recreation could have on our community and took it upon themselves to make it a priority," said Levi, who now works at Mi'kmaw Kina'matnewey as their Mi'kmaw Sports Performance Coordinator. "It's amazing somebody pays me to do this."

Levi said his experience working with NAIG can also be traced back several years. "When I first went to NAIG I was a participant, and I returned an advocate. The thing about NAIG is it's true: it's 50 percent about sport and 50 percent about culture, so it's a wonderful opportunity to showcase Mi'kmaw culture, while also helping to grow sport throughout all of Mi'kma'ki."

Rescheduled to July 2023 due to the 2020 pandemic, Levi expects the NAIG 2023 contingent of Mi'kmaw athletes, coaches, and managers to more than double compared to NAIG 2017, which took place in Toronto.

"It's a huge honour. And our people out West, our Indigenous brothers and sisters, they're going to see just how proud a Nation we are."

SELECT AWARDS & HONOURS

❋ Esso Award Winner for All-Star Goalie, 2020

❋ Nova Scotia Junior Hockey League Champion, 2017–2018

EVERETT SANIPASS
WORKING TOGETHER

Born: February 13, 1968
Elsipogtog First Nation, NB

The son of Joe and Marion (née Levi) Sanipass, Everett has a passion for sports that blossomed at a young age. "I learned a lot just following my dad around," Everett said, recalling how his father was active in both baseball and hockey. "I'd see him getting ready for the games and I'd attend his games, just watching everything unfold, so many great things in front of me."

By the time he'd reached his teens, scouts from both the American Hockey League and the American Baseball League were hoping to recruit young Everett.

SELECT AWARDS & HONOURS

❋ First New Brunswicker of First Nations heritage to play in the National Hockey League

❋ New Brunswick Sports Hall of Fame inductee, 2015

❋ Member of Canada's team at 1987 World Junior Tournament

❋ Drafted fourteenth overall in the 1986 NHL Entry Draft

❋ Played 164 NHL games with Chicago Blackhawks and Quebec Nordiques

"At fifteen years old, I had to make a decision: to either go full force into baseball or hockey," Everett said. "It was a trying time because I loved both sports dearly."

And while the Pittsburgh Pirates were prepared to send him to Triple A camps down south, Everett ultimately chose hockey.

"Just seeing how the people gather around at the arenas, that made my decision very clear," said Everett. "The support for hockey in Canada is amazing."

After being drafted fourteenth overall in the 1986 NHL draft, he was selected the next year to play with Team Canada at the World Junior Hockey Championships in Czechoslovakia. He began his NHL career that same year with the Chicago Blackhawks, where he remained as a forward until 1991, when he was traded to the Quebec Nordiques. He left the NHL soon after to play with the Halifax Citadels and then the NSJHL East Hants Penguins. He retired from hockey in 1995.

"My parents were always so supportive. Once they found out that I was interested in playing, they jumped on board with me and guided me the whole way."

A proud dad of six children, Everett only skates now if it's to help coach or mentor youth or for just a bit of "fun with the guys."

"It's time now for my generation to step up and pass the torch to our young ones, our children and grandchildren to come," he said. He hopes his example inspires other Indigenous youth to chase their dreams.

"I believe that any Indigenous person can make it to the most elite level of whatever area they choose. And you know all it takes? It just takes the right person to guide you," said Everett.

CHAD DENNY
BACK TO WHO WE ARE

Born: March 27, 1987
Eskasoni First Nation, NS

The son of Karen Denny and Noel Dennis Jr., Chad Denny was raised by his mother's parents, Dorothy and Douglas Denny, who he calls Mom and Dad. Under his grandparents' roof, there was just one steadfast rule: speak Mi'kmaw only. No more than six or seven when he first laced up a pair of skates, Chad was active in a variety of sports from a young age. "My father was also a good athlete. A lot of sports came naturally to me," he said.

As he grew older and his hockey talents became increasingly apparent, his grandfather sat him down. "You're not getting any younger—it's time we make a decision. If you want to keep at hockey, you have to show me some commitment."

And commit he did. At fifteen, Chad was drafted by the Lewiston MAINEiacs in the Quebec Major Junior Hockey League. He packed up his belongings to play with the MAINEiacs in Maine, USA, but because the American high school curriculum was different from Nova Scotia's, Chad had to continue his schooling through correspondence.

"It was pretty much, 'Here's an envelope: do this,' with no teacher," he said.

A kid alone in a new country, Chad struggled to stay on top of his schoolwork while also maintaining a strict practice regimen.

"When I was sixteen, seventeen years old, I'm like, 'Why am I doing this? What am I gonna do with an education?'"

But his Lewiston MAINEiacs coach, Clement Jodin, made sure Chad and the rest of his teammates kept their priorities straight. According to Chad, his coach always stressed the need for a backup plan. "He was always thinking of our futures. Basically, if we weren't at class that morning, we weren't playing that night," he said. "I'm forever grateful to him."

Chad managed to finish his high school credits remotely and, within a year of going pro, in 2008 he was assigned to the Chicago Wolves, who captured the American Hockey League title (Calder Cup) the same year. He also attended NHL camps with the Atlanta Thrashers and the Philadelphia Flyers, and played with the Utah Grizzlies and the Gwinnett Gladiators in another minor pro circuit, the East Coast Hockey League.

"To think, after all those years of playing pro, I was headed back to school," he said. "I was twenty-seven years old attending my first year of university."

On a full scholarship with the University of New Brunswick (UNB), Chad helped the team capture the Canadian University Hockey Championship in 2013, earning two bachelor degrees along the way. While at UNB, he argued for the right to submit his exit paper in his first language and won. Since graduating he's taught Mi'kmaw Immersion in both Quebec and New Brunswick schools and currently works as a language keeper for the Eel River Bar First Nation. And while Chad's achieved goals few hockey players dare to dream of, his only trace of pride comes from his Mi'kmaw roots. While his jerseys are all priceless collectables in hockey fandoms around the world, he's sent every one back home to his grandparents in Eskasoni. Today a father of two to Deacon and Meadow, Chad and his life partner, Tiffanie LaBillois—

a Mi'kmaw woman from Eel River Bar First Nation—are determined to raise their children with the Mi'kmaw traditions, values, and language they hold dear.

"I went fishing with him all day today. He loves to hunt and gather with us," Chad said, clearly proud of his son, Deacon Stone. The Denny family currently calls Eel River Bar First Nation their home. "He just loves nature, which is so great, because nature connects us back to who we are."

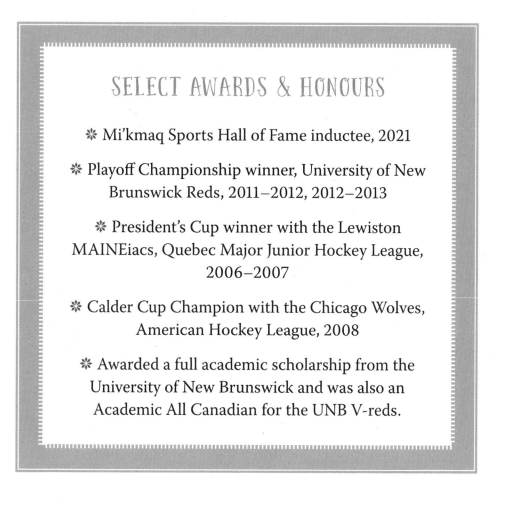

SELECT AWARDS & HONOURS

❋ Mi'kmaq Sports Hall of Fame inductee, 2021

❋ Playoff Championship winner, University of New Brunswick Reds, 2011–2012, 2012–2013

❋ President's Cup winner with the Lewiston MAINEiacs, Quebec Major Junior Hockey League, 2006–2007

❋ Calder Cup Champion with the Chicago Wolves, American Hockey League, 2008

❋ Awarded a full academic scholarship from the University of New Brunswick and was also an Academic All Canadian for the UNB V-reds.

SARA-LYNNE KNOCKWOOD
A BIG SISTER TO ALL

Born: December 12, 1985
Sipekne'katik, NS

"I think taekwondo was a bit of an accident," said Sara-Lynne Knockwood. Gifted at a range of sports at a young age, from rugby to soccer, she rose to become a world-renowned taekwondo athlete in her youth. "My sisters and I had gone to a boxing club in Sackville for a few years and then it shut down. So we were looking for something similar that was still close to home. It was my uncle who actually found this taekwondo club in Dartmouth. That was the beginning of a whole new story for us."

Raised by Ron and Jennifer (née Denny) Knockwood in Enfield, Nova Scotia, Sara-Lynne's dad, an RCMP officer, wanted his daughters to learn self-defence.

"We started training as white belts with [David] McKenna three times a week, and quickly advanced through the belt ranking system. The three of us, we all achieved our black belts at one point, and we just really enjoyed it."

Within months of taking up with David McKenna at his Dartmouth taekwondo club, Sara-Lynne was attending her first sanctioned World Taekwondo Federation Tournament in Moncton, NB, and won gold, going on to compete at the Pan American Games and Taekwondo World Championships. She was just sixteen years old.

Retiring from competition, Knockwood left for St. Francis Xavier University to earn a bachelor of science degree in human kinetics. After graduation, she went to work with Mi'kmaw Kina'matnewey (MK) as their Aboriginal Sport Project Coordinator. At MK, Sara-Lynne was responsible for coordinating the sporting events for Mi'kmaw communities across Nova Scotia. This role briefly overlapped with another—as a youth mentor with Sipekne'katik's Family and Children's Services. In the latter position, Sara-Lynne provided support and guidance to teenage girls on a weekly basis. Despite it being "truly one of the most rewarding positions I've ever had," after two years Sara-Lynne was forced to drop the extra work so she could focus on her master's degree full time.

Sara-Lynne attributes her success in school, sports, and career to the ongoing support of her family. Well aware of her good fortune, she's made it her mission to give back. Much to her credit, Sara-Lynne has helped open a taekwondo club in her hometown. An active volunteer with the Mi'kmaq Sport Council of Nova Scotia

SELECT AWARDS

* ❊ Gold, World Taekwondo Federation, 2006

* ❊ Gold, North American Indigenous Games (NAIG), Poomse-Senior division, 2006

* ❊ Silver, NAIG, Sparring—Senior division, 2006

* ❊ Gold, World Taekwondo Federation, 2002

* ❊ Gold, NAIG, Sparring—Junior division, 2002

* ❊ Gold, NAIG, Poomse—Junior division, 2002

* ❊ The National Tom Longboat Award, 2002

for several years, she's also served on various NAIG Committees as well as the Association of Canada's National Team Athletes and AthletesCan, to name a few.

These days, she's set most of her community efforts aside to focus on her own family. She and her partner Scott have their hands full raising three toddlers—two boys and one girl. She said she hopes just sharing her story inspires others to create their own.

"Nobody gets somewhere on their own, and you never know where someone will go. If no one was there to tell me about the taekwondo club, I may have never competed, and explored the countries that this sport has taken me to. So, I really think it's important to [share] stories and let kids know what opportunities are out there."

She also encourages everyone to continue growing, no matter how old they are.

"It's a scary thing to try something new, but if you don't, you won't know. Don't ever be afraid to say yes to something new. Because that's how you grow in the sport and how you grow as a person."

RICHARD PELLISSIER-LUSH
WEARER OF MANY HATS

Born: March 1989
Lennox Island First Nation, PEI

"I tried soccer, taekwondo, hockey…you name it, *all* the sports. My parents even put me in the Bantam Football program when I was a kid," Richard Pellissier-Lush said. "But I was a small, chubby boy and didn't like running very much. So after one season, I quit that too."

The son of Julie Pellissier-Lush (in case you didn't notice, one of this book's authors) and Rick Lush, Richard Pellissier-Lush was born in Winnipeg, Manitoba.

It wasn't until Grade 10 that, inspired by his best friend, a high school quarterback, Richard tried out for their school team

Amazing L'nu'k

and made the cut. Both were also being actively recruited by a Winnipeg street gang. Richard recalls his best friend saying, "Football is what we need to be focusing on."

And with that, Richard's path forward became clear.

"You're right, man. Let's go and practice," he said.

Later that same year, Richard and his mom returned to PEI to be closer to their Mi'kmaw roots. Picking up where he left off, he joined his high school football team, where he was soon scouted to play with the University of Manitoba. He returned to PEI a few years later to play for the Hurricanes at Holland College.

In 2006, he turned his eye to coaching.

"We started with three or four kids that were super interested in football, and worked our way from there," he said. Building on his young players' enthusiasm, Richard launched two tackle teams—the under-twelve Cornwall Timberwolves and, with Meagan Ferguson, the Island Demons female team—along with three First Nations teams: two flag teams in Scotchfort, and one in Lennox Island First Nation.

Richard, a cisgender male, said it's important for athletes to recognize that being sensitive is in fact a sign you're a strong and healthy person. "As Indigenous men, our sensitivities are our strengths. Elders in my community have taught me to see that tears are, in fact, medicine."

When he's not busy coaching football, Richard is busy being an activist, performer, social media influencer, writer, and young dad. He also dances regularly at **Mawio'mi'l** and other events. Richard is proud to share his culture, his stories, his drumming and traditions, but his passion shines through when he dances. This is shown in his spirit name, **Kitbu Amalkewinu** (Eagle Dancer).

"I wear many different hats, so every day looks different. I could be recruiting for a football team one day and speaking to a

Knowledge Keeper the next. More than anything, I consider myself an advocate for my people generally, and for youth specifically."

Whatever hat Richard chooses to wear, one thing's for certain: he wears it exceptionally well. Several young players, for example, say his coaching has helped them both on and off the field.

"He is the reason I keep playing football," a young PEI running back named Ethan told CBC. "I used to be scared of talking to people. Now I am part of the football community, I have more self-esteem to talk to everybody."

SELECT AWARDS & HONOURS

❉ Queen's Jubilee Platinum Award, 2023

❉ Heritage Recognition Award, PEI Department of Heritage, 2022

❉ National Indigenous Coaching Award, Aboriginal Sports Circle, 2020

❉ Lifetime Achievement Award, Sport PEI, 2020

❉ One of eight Indigenous youth selected to present to the Canadian Senate, 2019

❉ Marie Coyoteblanc Award for Indigenous Writing, 2018

❉ Valedictorian, Holland College, 2012

Amazing L'nu'k

TASHA MCKENZIE
A FEW GREAT WOMEN

Born: May 25, 1995
Sipekne'katik, NS

"The first time I stepped on the field, I played the entire game with a bit of rubber turf in my eye," Tasha McKenzie said, referencing her first game of rugby. "And I still managed to score a couple of tries, even though I'd never even seen the sport before."

Tasha was approached right after that first game by a coach for the Women's Rugby Nova Scotia Team, who invited her to join them for practice. Brushing the invitation off as "too good to be true," she ended up joining them on the field a year later—as a Grade 10 student at Hants East Rural High School. "I actually had to get special permission back then because I was the youngest person on the team."

Raised on the reservation by a single mom, Patricia McKenzie, with help from her grandmother and great aunt, Tasha said she owes much of her success in life to rugby and a few strong Mi'kmaw women.

"I was bullied a lot as a kid. My hair was too frizzy for the Natives and too straight for the Blacks," Tasha said, who is Mi'kmaw and Black. "Sport is what saved me from being an addict or going to jail like my older brother. If it wasn't for sport, I don't know where I'd be."

With her mom unable to drive her to practice, an older player, Sara-Lynne Knockwood, did. "She would go out of her way, taking me to practice and making sure she got me home after. Sara-Lynne was incredible."

Tasha's grandmother Dorothy McKenzie made sure she was a proud young Mi'kmaw woman. "She was my biggest fan. She lost a lot of her language back at the Indian Day School, but she taught me everything she could remember," said Tasha. "And no matter what was going on, she always made it out to watch my games. It's kind of weird to play without her."

With her grandmother's support, Tasha continued to excel and became the All-Star at the Atlantic University Sport Women's Rugby in 2013. Following in Sara-Lynne's footsteps, she enrolled at St. Francis Xavier University and hopes to begin her education degree after finishing her bachelor of arts.

"I used to see [being biracial] as a barrier. Now I see it as a privilege. As a coach and an athlete, I'm able to reach both communities, whereas someone who's just one may only be able to reach one. And that's rare," said Tasha. "I hope to reach someone like me, who found sport, and it completely changed their life."

A recent graduate of the Sports Nova Scotia Black and Indigenous Coaching Mentorship program, Tasha's goal is to be a BIPOC role model both on the field and in the classroom. "I think it's important we have others to look up to everywhere."

And it looks like she's well on her way. For ten years, Tasha was a rugby coach for the Hants East Rural High School and in 2021, she helped coach the under-eighteen Keltics. Now she works as a referee, and she says this new role has given her "a whole new appreciation for [her] favourite sport."

MYKEO PARKER-CHRISTMAS
ONE BOY'S DREAM

Born: March 12, 2002
Membertou First Nation, NS

"I remember many trips to Membertou, getting to go to powwows while we were there," Mykeo Parker-Christmas said of his childhood. "And when we'd go back to Halifax, I had this little handmade drum...you know, with the four corners painted on it...and I used to drum away on it, just like I was back there."

The son of Nicola Parker and Bernd Christmas, Mykeo also played a lot of soccer as a kid.

"As soon as I could walk, my older brother and I, we were playing soccer," said Mykeo. "Every chance we got, we'd just be out there, kicking that ball everywhere, chasing it into the bushes, just having fun."

It wasn't until high school, however, that Mykeo's Mi'kmaw upbringing and his passion for soccer would finally collide.

"To have my whole Membertou family watching, and then to actually win the provincials," he said, recalling winning the high school provincial championship as part of the Halifax Citadels on Cape Breton University's soccer field, "it was a pretty special game."

Shortly after, Mykeo was offered a full scholarship to play college-level soccer in Tennessee. After he made the 3,000-kilometre trek in the fall of 2020 to start his first semester with the University of Memphis, the COVID-19 pandemic not only forced the National

Collegiate Athletic Association (NCAA) to delay soccer season, but it also prevented Mykeo from returning to Canada. Prior to the pandemic, Mykeo said he and his family travelled to Membertou at least once every two months.

"If it wasn't for my team, it would have been a lot harder," said Mykeo. And while he found a second family in his teammates, he said playing soccer at the NCAA level has been a huge adjustment. Before the NCAA, he was often the strongest player on his team.

These days, not so much.

"Everyone here is a bull," he said. "I really have to put everything into it. But committing to this, a division-one school in the NCAA, it's always been a goal of mine."

Committed to reaching his goals, Mykeo urges others to act on their dreams, too.

"Never ever fall short on yourself. As long as you put your heart and mind to it and dedicate yourself, anything can happen. Always dream the biggest you can."

SELECT AWARDS & HONOURS

❋ Dean's List, University of Memphis, 2020–2021

❋ Full Soccer Scholarship, National Collegiate Athletic Association (NCAA), University of Memphis, 2020

❋ Golden Boot Award, Toyota U-15 National Soccer Championships, 2017

PART IV
EDUCATORS & KNOWLEDGE KEEPERS

People just do not realize the importance of our language. People do not realize that in our language...there's no such thing as a 'he' or a 'she' or an 'it.' Our language speaks of things that are alive—trees, fish, animals, people, and even rock. It's so beautiful when you understand it. And it tells you—our language tells you so much that sometimes it's unbelievable.

–Kji-keptin **Alexander Denny**, Eskasoni First Nation

Knowledge is held by the spirits, shared by the spirits, and comes from the spirits...our body then can be seen as the carrier of the learning spirit.

–Elder **Danny Musqua**, the Saulteaux Keeseekoose First Nation

Determination played a big role for a lot of people to make it all work, to make sure that the church never got its dirty paws on our school again. And our people now, when they finish high school, they can go out to do whatever they want. That's part of the master plan, to educate as many as possible.

–Saqamaw **Mi'sel Joe**, Miawpukek First Nation

DID YOU KNOW?

Respect for the life cycle of nature can be found in the way L'nu'k talk to one another. Unlike the English language, which is noun-based and primarily speaks of objects, the Mi'kmaw language is verb-based. This means the Mi'kmaq naturally describe things according to what they do and how they interrelate and interact with other aspects of the world. For example, in Mi'kmaw, the word for toboggan is **tepaqn***, which means "to drag along the ground"—exactly what you do with a toboggan. Another example is the insect* **glmuej***, a mosquito, which is described as "the one that sings before she bites you."*

ELDER ELSIE CHARLES BASQUE
THE GREATEST GIFT

Born: May 12, 1916; Died: April 11, 2016
Hectanooga, NS

lsie was just three years old when she was left in the care of her only sibling, then thirteen-year-old Lucy Marie. Her mother, Margaret, soon abandoned the family after her father, Joe Charles, was diagnosed with tuberculosis. When her father returned with a clean bill of health after three years in hospital, he began earning for his family again as a wilderness guide to wealthy American tourists. According to Elsie, her father (she would call him "Papa" well into her adult years) would often say, "To be somebody, one needs a good education." Under her father's care,

Elsie was taught the importance of learning, along with things like how to trap minks and weasels, build canoes, and shoot a rifle.

In 1929, after reading about the "great education" a new forward-thinking school planned to offer all L'nu'k, Joe enrolled his then thirteen-year-old daughter to attend Shubenacadie Residential School. Among the first to attend, Elsie entered Shubenacadie with a Grade 8 education, only to leave two years later—with a Grade 8 education.

"What had I learned in those 29 months? How to darn a sock, sew a straight seam on the sewing machine, and how to scrub clothes on a washboard," she later told *The Halifax Herald*.

In spite of Shubenacadie, Elsie proceeded to earn her high school diploma and enroll at Truro's teachers' college, where she became class president and was awarded for her skills in debating. Graduating in 1937, she became the first Mi'kmaw person to earn a teacher's license, and, shortly after, the first Mi'kmaw person to teach at a non-Native school.

In 1939 she established Shubenacadie's first Indian Day School for one reason—so local children could return home to their families after school. She married Isaac Basque two years later and continued to run the day school until 1947, when the Department of Indian Affairs took it over. Elsie was immediately dismissed and replaced by the Sisters of Charity, the same nuns responsible for administering to the students of Shubenacadie Residential School.

Determined to move forward, in 1951 Elsie and Isaac packed up their four children and headed to Boston, where Elsie established a preschool for Indigenous children and night classes for Indigenous adults with support from the city's Indian Council. While there Elsie also initiated a sort of "meals on wheels" nutritional and transportation service as well as a variety of Indigenous-themed social and cultural gatherings for local Elders. Emerging in America as a National Spokeswoman for Indigenous Elders, Elsie was frequently called upon to deliver guest lectures at universities, colleges, and public organizations.

"My mother believed you could be anything you wanted to be," her daughter Marty told the *Globe and Mail*. "She wanted others to believe in themselves."

After retiring in 1983, Elsie returned to Nova Scotia, and, ten years later, met with some of her surviving students for a Shubenacadie Indian Day School Reunion in 1993. She later described this reunion as the "most heartwarming experience of my life."

"They came back to say thank you," Elsie told *The Herald*. "It's the greatest gift a teacher could ask for."

Elsie passed away peacefully in 2016, one month and one day shy of her hundredth birthday.

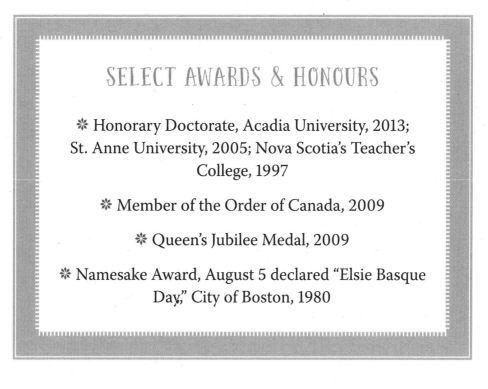

SELECT AWARDS & HONOURS

❋ Honorary Doctorate, Acadia University, 2013; St. Anne University, 2005; Nova Scotia's Teacher's College, 1997

❋ Member of the Order of Canada, 2009

❋ Queen's Jubilee Medal, 2009

❋ Namesake Award, August 5 declared "Elsie Basque Day," City of Boston, 1980

ALICE MITCHELL
WELCOMING THE CHILDREN

Born: March 1852; Died: June 1924
Rocky Point, PEI

Born the same year Prince Edward Island's Free Education Act was passed, an act which granted all PEI children—including the Mi'kmaq—free and equal access to an education, Alice Mitchell inherited her occupation and home. Part of a long line of "coopers" (an old-fashioned English term used to describe those who make and sell things like barrels, buckets, and baskets out of wood), Alice and her brother Louis continued the coopering tradition from the same home on the same land passed down to them for generations. Then one day in 1912, the two siblings received an eviction notice. According to the notice, their land—near present-day Rocky Point Reserve in Epekwitk, PEI—was theirs no more. It had been purchased by a white farmer, and they were required to leave immediately.

Cruel by anyone's standards today, the racist laws of the day prevented Alice and her brother from taking legal action: back then, any lawyer found working with a Mi'kmaw person was immediately stripped of their ability to practice law. Nonetheless, someone was sympathetic enough to help Alice draft a letter in the English language to send to the federal Department of Indian Affairs. The letter was apparently persuasive enough to motivate the department to approach the farmer and ask for some mercy. Yet even with the government on their side, the farmer refused.

As a compromise, the department instead purchased three acres close by in 1914. Known as the Rocky Point Reserve, those three acres became the home of many displaced L'nu'k in PEI. In fact, within a year so many Mi'kmaw families had descended upon those three little acres that Alice asked the local Indian agent to write Indian Affairs in Ottawa once more. This time, she had a plan in mind to relay.

The PEI Indian Agent wrote:

"[The children] are running wild and she cannot keep them under control at all. She also informs me that there is a man on the reserve who is a fairly good scholar and would teach there for the term if you could get him a small salary from the government. Alice herself will supply the house."

The Rocky Point Day School was launched in October 1915, and true to her word, Alice welcomed these schoolchildren into her home. Moving to its own building in 1916, the school thrived for seven years, closing permanently in 1922 due to a lack of students, after several families moved away.

KJI-KEPTIN ALEXANDER DENNY
SIAWI-L'NUI'SULTIK

Born: July 26, 1940; Died: December 25, 2004
Eskasoni First Nation, NS

Born to a young Mi'kmaw woman, Alex Denny was taken in as an infant by Elders Andrew and Mary Anne Denny. Raising him as their own, they regaled their son with bedtime stories in their mother tongue. Far from *Goldilocks and the Three Bears* or *Goodnight Moon*, the tales these Elders told were often true—stories containing Mi'kmaw oral history, as well as Mi'kmaw prayers and, of course, Mi'kmaw legends. Alex would later claim these stories laid the foundation for his lifelong commitment to knowledge keeping on his Nation's behalf.

Already determined at fourteen, Alex sought to further his education, travelling to Chatham, New Brunswick, for boarding school and later to Charlottetown, PEI, for high school. He left in Grade 11, returning to Eskasoni after learning his father, Andrew Denny, had fallen ill. He later earned his GED before heading to business school. After marrying his childhood sweetheart, Janet Paul, in the early 1960s, the two settled in Eskasoni to raise their children—all fluent Mi'kmaw speakers to this day.

By 1966, recognizing his leadership potential, community Elders appointed Alex to the lifelong role of Kji-keptin of the Sante' Mawio'mi (Grand Captain of the Mi'kmaw Grand Council)—a clear sign of the respect he'd already earned from the community, even as a young man.

SELECT AWARDS & HONOURS

❋ Mi'kmaq Sports Hall of Fame inductee, 2017

❋ Namesake award established, the Kji-Keptin Alex Denny Memorial Sports/Education Scholarship Award, 2006

❋ Appointed by Mi'kmaw Elders to lifelong role of Kji-keptin of the Sante' Mawio'mi (Grand Captain of the Grand Council), 1966

❋ Tom Longboat Award, 1959

A few years later, Alex and other like-minded Mi'kmaq came together to secure political leadership for their Nation, and, in 1969, the Union of Nova Scotia Indians (UNSI) became a reality. With Alex as president, UNSI lobbied the Government of Canada to recognize the Mi'kmaw treaties, and, by the 1980s, Canada declared October 1 Treaty Day. That same decade, Alex and UNSI took their Nation's right to self-government to the international stage. As a result, the Mi'kmaq Nation became the first Indigenous Nation in the world to have its linguistic and political rights recognized by the United Nations. Around the same time, Alex also helped establish the Mi'kmaq Resource Centre at Cape Breton University (CBU), known today as Unama'ki College. Years later, when Unama'ki College opened its doors in 2012 to their first

Mi'kmaw language lab, it was named "Kji-keptin Alexander Denny L'nui'sultimkeweyo'kuom" (Grand Captain Alexander Denny Language Lab) in his honour.

"Alex was very much an advocate of immersion in our schools. Oftentimes he'd walk into our offices, telling me that he was speaking in schools and how we should be doing more to promote the Mi'kmaw language," Eleanor Bernard, former executive director of the Mi'kmaw Kina'matnewey, said.

With his passing in 2004, his eldest son, Andrew Denny, inherited the role of Kji-keptin Sante' Mawio'mi. Along with countless other Mi'kmaw leaders, Andrew continues to execute his father's vision to this day.

And while Alex left this world for the Spirit World in 2004, his impact continues to reverberate throughout all of Mi'kma'ki. The phrase he repeated throughout his lifetime can be found etched on his tombstone:

Siawi-l'nui'sultik, it reads, which translates to "continue speaking Mi'kmaw."

ELDER DANIEL PAUL
A MAN OF HIS WORD

Born: December 5, 1938
Sipekne'katik First Nation, NS

"I was around sixteen, and I was working at a hat factory in Boston, and a Black lady working there, from either Louisiana or Mississippi, she calls me over one day," Elder Daniel N. Paul said. "She says, 'Boy, you walk around here with your head hanging down, as if you think all these white guys are better than you…Exactly what do you know about your own culture?' And I said, 'I know very little.' 'Well,' she says, "Why don't you learn a lot about it? Maybe you'll wind up being very proud of your history."'

Born in 1938 on Indian Brook Indian Reserve to William and Sarah (née Noel) Paul, Daniel was ejected from school two years before that conversation at the hat factory—after his school's principal, a Catholic priest, escorted young Daniel off the school's grounds by his shirt collar for refusing to rewrite a math exam for which he'd already received 100 percent. Daniel was finally free of the very school that taught him he descended "from an inferior race of savages."

And so, his real education began.

Ten years later, in 1965, Daniel and a couple other L'nu'k were gathered in a Halifax pub enjoying a beer when Daniel glanced up, noticing a replica of the 1749 scalping proclamation on the tavern's wall. Issued by then Nova Scotia Governor Edward Cornwallis, the proclamation offered a reward of ten guineas for every Mi'kmaw person taken or killed. Having long thought the scalping bounties were more rumour than fact, Daniel could now read one, word for word, in person. He felt sick to his stomach, and he had proof. Proof that the genocide of the Mi'kmaq had been the original intent of the colonial government.

This and other real-world educational moments led Daniel to commit his life to "writing the wrongs" of his people. While he sought out employment over the years that aligned with this goal, such as his work as Saqamaw of the Shubenacadie District and Justice of the Peace for Nova Scotia, Daniel used his free time to carefully research his people's history. These countless hours of research eventually led him to write his most famous book, *We Were Not the Savages: A Mi'kmaw Perspective on the Collision between European and Native American Civilizations.*

Published in 1993 and now in its fourth edition, Daniel's book has sold tens of thousands of copies worldwide. Prior to *We Were Not the Savages*, it was common for historians and educators to downplay or even deny the violence inflicted on the Mi'kmaq. According to Indigenous Studies professor and activist Dr. Pam Palmater, "It is literally the book that every Indigenous student and academic all over Turtle Island should read."

In February 2018, when the City of Halifax finally tore down the statue of Governor Edward Cornwallis, Daniel—who'd tirelessly campaigned for its removal—celebrated by standing in the rubble of where it once stood.

"I think it's a sign of progress when you see something like this happen in any city in Canada," he said. "I hope in the future that this park gets a new name. I would suggest 'Peace and Friendship Park.'" And guess what? That's exactly what it's named today.

Now eighty-four, Daniel continues to work tirelessly to eradicate ignorance, uphold Mi'kma'ki, and educate the public. The fourth edition of *We Were Not the Savages* was released on September 30, 2022.

SELECT AWARDS, HONOURS & PUBLICATIONS

❋ *The Hidden Histories of the Americas*, 2011;
We Were Not the Savages, 1993

❋ Wel-lukwen (loosely translated to "he done good")
Award, Nova Scotia Human Rights Commission,
2022.

❋ Torch Bearer Award, Sri Chinmoy Peace Run, 2018

❋ Honorary Doctorate of Laws, Dalhousie University,
2013

❋ Grand Chief Donald Marshall Senior Memorial
Elder Award, 2007

❋ Multicultural Education Council of Nova Scotia
Award, 2007

❋ Member of the Order of Canada, 2005

❋ Member of the Order of Nova Scotia, 2002

❋ Honorary Doctor of Letters,
University of Sainte-Anne, 1997

ELDER BERNIE FRANCIS
THE RETURN OF MAYFLOWERS

Membertou First Nation, NS

"There is nothing that smells better than a mayflower. It smells absolutely beautiful," Bernie Francis told Trudy Sable. "I still remember picking bunches with my father and then binding them with a twine." Bernie goes on to explain how each summer in his youth, he and his dad hand-harvested mayflowers by the bundle—as well as wild blueberries, strawberries, raspberries, and blackberries—to later sell for profit.

Along with learning to harvest and gather sustainably, Bernie owes his early lessons as a Mi'kmaw language keeper to his father and a handful of other Elders. "[Every] time I saw a certain group of men, older men, standing around talking, I would immediately run to those people and stand next to them just so I could, you know, listen to them. And they'd tease the bejesus out of one another about their language," said Bernie, who also quickly picked up on the many humorous nuances and double-entendres of his mother tongue.

Having also mastered the English language, Bernie picked up work as a bilingual translator in the early 1970s, representing fellow L'nu'k during federal court proceedings. He quickly became aware of how few Mi'kmaw translators, even proficient speakers, existed. So when the late Dr. Peter Christmas, then director of the Mi'kmaq Association of Cultural Studies, approached him to see if he'd help preserve the Mi'kmaw language, Bernie was all in. In 1974, he left his job with the courts and began studying linguistics at the University of Toronto, where he and fellow linguist Dr. Doug Smith set about developing a Mi'kmaw orthography, a kind of dictionary.

Over the next six years they gradually identified seventeen letters in the Mi'kmaw alphabet—eleven consonants and six vowels—and standardized spelling conventions. Launched in 1980, the Smith/Francis orthography is now widely accepted by L'nu'k throughout Nova Scotia, Newfoundland and Labrador, Prince Edward Island, and parts of New Brunswick.

Since the launch of the orthography, Bernie has served as a national Mi'kmaw representative to international media, governments, and academics, while authoring and co-authoring countless peer-reviewed scholarly articles, books, university lectures, and public presentations. Even so, he likely values his work with the Mi'kmaw children most.

✳ Honorary Doctorate, Saint Mary's University, 2018; Dalhousie University, 1999

✳ *Mi'kmaw Grammar of Father Pacifique*, 2017

✳ Co-author, *The Language of This Land, Mi'kma'ki*, shortlisted for the Atlantic Book Award for Scholarly Writing, 2013

✳ Co-Creator, the *Ta'n Weji-sqalia'tiek Mi'kmaw Place Names Digital Atlas and Website Project*, 2010

"It's not the Elders that carry the language, it's the children," he said. The catch, however—the real challenge—is engaging the child. "We have to make it so that it's interesting for the child, that way they will actually pay attention."

To this end, Bernie has transcribed many popular songs and poems from English into Mi'kmaw. Just one example is *Ninen Na Mi'kma'ji'jk*—a musical collection of children's songs and rhymes in Mi'kmaw. Featuring traditional Mi'kmaw songs alongside translations of popular nursery rhymes like "Twinkle, Twinkle, Little Star" and "Eensy Weensy Spider," the CD also contains *Weska'qelmut Apje'juanu*, the Mi'kmaw translation of

Sheree Fitch's children's book *Kisses Kisses Baby-O!* Bernie's also translated a children's story by Angela Jeffrey, *The Purple Frog*, into *Nisqnanamuksit sqolj*.

"I grew up with stories as a kid, those legends that are still bouncing around in my head," he said. "There was a coherence to them. I wanted to ensure that when this is read, it will have the same effect as the old stories had on me."

Just as Bernie learned to harvest the mayflowers and berries so that they return plentifully next season, he's also helped preserve the language of the Mi'kmaq so it will be spoken for generations to come.

SAQAMAW MI'SEL JOE
SELF DETERMINATION

Born: June 4, 1947
Miawpukek First Nation, NL

Born in 1947 on Miawpukek First Nation, Ktaqmkuk, into a Mi'kmaw tradition of leadership, both Mi'sel Joe's grandfather and uncle held the office of hereditary Saqamaw, while his great-great-uncle, Morris Lewis, was the first ever appointed Chief in Newfoundland by the Grand Chief in Mi'kmaw territory.

"Back when I was young, people lived off the land. Our history, our culture, was strong," Mi'sel said. As a child, Mi'sel grew up attending school in his home community. However, after Grade 8, he refused to attend Indian Day School in the nearby community of St. Alban's. Forced to earn his keep, he became his father's apprentice, helping him chop lumber for the local mill. Two years later, unable to keep up with his dad, who "cut five to six cords of wood a day with a bucksaw," he left for the mainland with just fifty dollars in his pocket. He spent his first night away in a Halifax rooming house, where he was dealt his first blow of racism. He remembers being asked, "What kind of an Indian are you? I thought we killed all you guys." Mi'sel left with his cousin for Toronto shortly after, where he began to work a series of temporary jobs. From farmhand to underground miner, railroad worker to heavy equipment operator, he said, "Every job I could find, I wanted to try it. I wouldn't change that experience for anything. It's good education and I think it's good for the soul."

Finally returning home in 1974, Mi'sel brought his off-reserve experiences to politics, first as a band councillor, and after his uncle's passing, as Miawpukek's Traditional Saqamaw and Newfoundland District Chief for the Mi'kmaq Grand Council. In 1983, shortly after taking on the roles, he and his community were dealt a blow. The Government of Newfoundland tried to go back on its promise to provide their community with its annual funding of $800,000. Undaunted, he and the Miawpukek L'nu'k fought back.

"We knew that if we returned to Conne River without the funding we would be beaten forever. The hunger strike was our only option left and it worked."

After weeks of negotiations and eight days of a publicly staged hunger strike by Mi'sel and eight other L'nu'k, the government finally gave in, and a legal agreement was created, requiring all future funding go directly to the Conne River Band.

SELECT AWARDS, HONOURS & PUBLICATIONS

✳ Co-author, *My Indian*, Breakwater Books, 2021

✳ *Muinji'j Ji'nmus'sit*, Breakwater Books, 2003; *Muinji'j Becomes a Man*, Breakwater Books, 2003

✳ Member of the Order of Canada, 2017

✳ Honorary Doctor of Laws, Memorial University of Newfoundland & Labrador, 2004

With that, Mi'sel's fate was sealed, and he would go on to lead Miawpukek from isolation and poverty into prosperity. Part of the team in the 1980s that won Miawpukek recognition as a status band under the Indian Act, he also ensured the community took charge of their own schools in 1985.

"Today we have 100 percent employment within the community. We've got a number of partnerships with big businesses. It took a lot of good people to get here. And the best reward of all that is to go into the school and see young kids in the school being taught the language, the history."

When Newfoundland and Labrador finally decided in 1997 to stop separating their children into either Protestant- or Catholic-run schools, the church's grip was further loosened, and the dream of the language's return slowly rekindled. Today, students at Se't A'newey Kina'matino'kuom (St. Anne's School) in Miawpukek First Nation spend a few hours a week learning to read and write the Mi'kmaw language.

Nonetheless, Mi'sel said there's still plenty to do.

"We have to educate everybody. That shouldn't be our job, but it is at this stage. And we need to do more."

DR. MARIE BATTISTE
THE LEARNING SPIRIT

Born: 1949
Potlotek First Nation, NS,
and the Aroostook Mi'kmaq Nation, ME

In 1947, young parents John and Annie Battiste left Eskasoni First Nation in search of work, finding it in the potato- and blueberry-producing fields of Maine. The last of their four children, Marie Battiste was born in Houlton, Maine, where the family settled and where they were known to host new families arriving south of the border.

"There was no highway yet, so anybody who came across the border went by our street. My parents were known as who you'd stop to see. They'd offer food, coffee, whatever was needed," Marie said. "Sometimes I lost my clothing to somebody who'd come through and didn't have anything. My mother was one of those people who said, 'You give away a dime, it'll always come back.'"

While Marie's parents had very little education, they did have hope for what education might hold for their children's future. They spoke their L'nu language, hoping it would have a role in that future. "My father always said to me that I was special. And when you're told by a parent that you're special, you believe it, in your heart. And he thought I was special because I was born in the United States. [He] knew that I had an inheritance that came with that. But he didn't know what that would be," Marie said.

Coming of age in the 1960s, Marie would witness America's civil rights movement firsthand, committing entire sections of Martin

Luther King's "I have a dream" speech to her memory. "Racism, inequality, systemic discrimination, learning from Martin Luther King and the civil rights movement how to make changes—all of these have been inspiring, motivating events in my life," she said.

As her first job out of university, she was tasked with introducing the new preschool program "Head Start" to children from three of Maine's Native American communities. She went on to teach Vietnam war vets and disadvantaged youth basic language and arithmetic skills at University of Maine at Farmington, in its Program of Basic Studies. At twenty-four, she was accepted at Harvard University, where she met then-law student James (Sa'ke'j) Youngblood Henderson, "my hero and the love of my life," graduating a year later with her master's in education. She went on to further studies at Stanford University, becoming the first L'nu to receive a doctorate. Marie was then invited to work in Potlotek First Nation with her family, where she pioneered a Mi'kmaw language and culture curriculum at the local school. In 1993, when the language program was secure, Marie, Sa'ke'j and their three children left for Saskatchewan, where Marie became faculty with the University of Saskatchewan, teaching for the next three decades in Indigenous education.

And while Marie's ivy-league status and hard work continue to earn a great deal of attention, she claims her own motivations have always been deeply spiritual. "I went to Harvard and Stanford and so on...While I think that that has a measure of success, it is not the success that I ultimately wanted." Rather, she describes the Indigenous concept of "the learning spirit."

"In terms of Indigenous ways of knowing, the Elders say we don't come into this world alone. We come with learning spirits that guide and support us so that we may [enter] into a continuous learning process." And while she said we may encounter challenges that cause us to falter and forget, or "hide our learning spirit and our purpose for being here," we can recover this spirit—by learning our own gifts and purpose for them. Hers was to expand the Mi'kmaw language, the teachings of Elders, and our knowledge of the interconnectedness of relationships. "We need to help people nourish their learning spirits."

After retiring from her long-time faculty position at the University of Saskatchewan, Marie and her partner Sa'ke'j moved back to Cape Breton in 2021. In her new position at Cape Breton University, Marie is focused on helping the university "decolonize the academy"—and helping the faculty and students nourish their learning spirits.

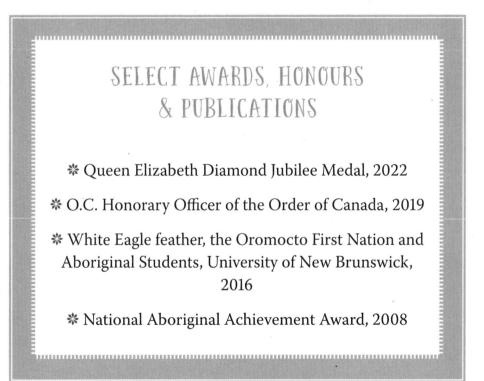

SELECT AWARDS, HONOURS & PUBLICATIONS

❋ Queen Elizabeth Diamond Jubilee Medal, 2022

❋ O.C. Honorary Officer of the Order of Canada, 2019

❋ White Eagle feather, the Oromocto First Nation and Aboriginal Students, University of New Brunswick, 2016

❋ National Aboriginal Achievement Award, 2008

ELDER GERALD GLOADE
NO AMOUNT OF GOLD

Millbrook First Nation, NS

Raised primarily by his grandmother, Gerald Gloade is the son of Millbrook's first elected Chief, Gerald Gloade (Senior), and Mary Bridget Gloade. Because he was born with a heart condition, rather than playing with kids his own age, Gerald spent most his youth listening to his grandmother tell traditional Mi'kmaw stories. "I just wouldn't have the knowledge I have today without my time with her," he said.

Taking root, those stories helped Gerald grow to become a gifted artist and storyteller himself. Hired straight out of the Truro Vocational School to do graphic design for the province, Gerald's storytelling gifts quickly became apparent, and he was reassigned work in education, soon sharing his culture's oral history with audiences of all ages. In 2005 he was handpicked to help develop programs for the Mi'kmawey Debert Cultural Centre, which showcases ancient Mi'kmaw artifacts from communities throughout Nova Scotia. Nearly every year since, Gerald has illustrated the Cultural Centre's highly anticipated "Mi'kmaw Month Posters," all the while educating multiple audiences—from kindergarten students to university professors—through a wide range of demonstrations, presentations, and nature tours.

"When you hear a story in the Mi'kmaw language, it creates images. It shows you these pictures. It's only there in my head [and] it's like, 'I've got to get it out…If I don't paint something I'm going to explode'" he said in a video for the centre, laughing. "And that's

SELECT AWARDS, HONOURS & PUBLICATIONS

❋ "Creatures of the North" Coin Design Contest, Royal Canadian Mint, 2020

❋ Illustrator, *Jujijk: Mi'kmaw Insects,* 2019

❋ "My Canada, My Inspiration" Coin Design Contest, Royal Canadian Mint, 2017

❋ Finalist, Portia White Prize, 2011

❋ Featured Artist, Vancouver Olympics, 2009

what I love to do. Just like, put images to the imagery that's created from a story."

Art from comics like *Captain America, Iron Man, Thor, The Hulk,* and *X-Men* are his biggest influences, and Gerald loves to use art to tell a story. Remarkably, his "storytelling artwork" can even be found in his award-winning Royal Canadian Mint designs. "The beaver was our first currency, we traded beaver pelts," the Knowledge Keeper told CBC. His artwork for the winning silver beaver coin manages to commemorate Canada's 150th anniversary while also honouring the Mi'kmaq's long-established history of trade—one that came along well before the currency used for trade now, or even the establishment of the country "Canada."

Finally, as author of "The Beaver Dam Community Wellness Study," Gerald also harnesses his storytelling skills to help save the real-life land and water of his Millbrook First Nation home. The study objects to the development of a new open-pit gold mine, outlining how it would permanently destroy the land and habitat where the people of the Millbrook First Nation hunt and gather. "Our rights are protected, and that way of life must be protected. [Those] are things you cannot replace for any amount of gold," Gerald said.

After asking his father how he came by his creativity, Gerald's dad responded, "You got it from the Creator, so don't waste it."

Using those talents to preserve as much of Mi'kma'ki as he can for future generations could be considered Gerald's life's mission.

"That's what it's all about—the kids. They're what's left after we're gone."

THE HONOURABLE JAIME BATTISTE
THE BOXER

Born: 1979

Potlotek First Nation, NS

"This is for all the youth out there who doubted themselves because of where they're from or what their background was," the newly elected member of parliament (MP) for Sydney-Victoria said after winning his seat.

The son of Indigenous scholars Marie Battiste and James (Sa'ke'j) Youngblood Henderson, Jaime (pronounced "hi-may") Battiste recalls discussing the treaties as a child with his parents at the kitchen table. While eventually he fought for the rights of all Indigenous people in Canada, Jaime learned to box as a boy at the Sydney Boxing Club. It seems even with scholars for parents, Jaime knew he had to fight to beat the odds.

"When I was growing up on a reserve, there was a greater chance I would have died a violent death or committed suicide than get a nomination for the federal party," he said.

Elected to his Cape Breton riding in 2019, he became the first Mi'kmaq to be elected to Parliament, and the first parliamentarian to speak Mi'kmaw in the House of Commons. Prior to becoming an MP, Jaime actively worked to make positive change for all of Mi'kma'ki, especially Mi'kmaw youth. Putting those childhood dinner conversations to good use, in 2015 Jaime became lead Treaty Educator with the Mi'kmaw education authority Mi'kmaw Kina'matnewey (MK).

Two years later, MK reported that the graduation rate of Mi'kmaw high school students had shot from 30 to 90 percent compared to twenty years prior—giving Mi'kma'ki the distinction of having the highest on-reserve graduation rate in the country.

And despite this, perhaps Jaime's proudest achievement so far was his federal funding announcement delivered in February 2022, when he shared that over one million dollars will be allocated to Mi'kmaw Kina'matnewey to help revitalize the Mi'kmaw language.

"We have so many great language champions and so many great language warriors in our communities, we've come such a long way," said Jaime.

While he presently calls Eskasoni First Nation home, it appears Jaime's work in Ottawa has only just begun. Winning his seat again in 2021, he was appointed Parliamentary Secretary to the Minister of Crown-Indigenous Relations the same year.

"I learned as a boxer in the Sydney Boxing Club with Brad Ross, fight until it's over...and never stop until it's over."

SELECT AWARDS & HONOURS

❋ Sovereign's Medal for Volunteers, 2018

❋ Founding member, Mi'kmaq-Maliseet Atlantic Youth Council (MMAYC), 2016

❋ Named as one of the "National Aboriginal Role Models in Canada," National Aboriginal Health Organization, 2005

PART V

TWO-EYED SEEING SCIENTISTS & DIGITAL MEDIA TECHSPLORERS

It's only in the last few years that they're realizing that Indigenous knowledge is way ahead in terms of solutions and answers...And after thousands of years, Western science is slowly starting to catch up.

–Two-Eyed Seeing Scientist **Jennifer Sylliboy**, Eskasoni First Nation

I have full respect for traditional medicines in combination with the Westernized medicine. My personal belief is in the use of traditional Indigenous drum and song. It deeply touches the soul. It gives me strength to get through difficult things... it is my medicine that has always made laser-focused. It is my medicine that makes me a better doctor.

–Emergentologist and Anesthesiologist **Dr. Rob Johnson**, Millbrook First Nation

For those currently interested in STEM related fields right now, studying, trying to get through. I'm saying just think about something amazing that you could possibly do in the future with what you're working on right now. Because the opportunities are limitless.

–Mechanical Engineer **Jordan Alexander**, Qalipu First Nation

NETUKULIMK AND ETUAPTMUMK

Netukulimk is an essential concept of the Mi'kmaq that grounds each person in an equally responsible, interconnected web of relationships between all living and non-living things on the planet. It focuses on living sustainably by wasting nothing and taking only what's necessary. It's the foundation of the spiritual connection between the Mi'kmaq and the natural environment.

A term coined by Mi'kmaw Elder Albert Marshall, **Etuaptmumk** (or in English, Two-Eyed Seeing) emphasizes the importance of integrating multiple ways of knowing into one's world view and belief systems, rather than just one.

ELDERS MURDENA
AND ALBERT MARSHALL
A COMBINED VISION

Murdena Marshall: Born: September 17, 1942; Died: October 22, 2018.
We'koqma'q First Nation, NS

Albert Marshall: Born: 1938
Eskasoni First Nation, NS

Born and raised on the We'koqma'q reserve, Murdena Marie Marshall was only eight when her mother died and her father sent her to live with her maternal grandparents. Soon after she moved in, Murdena's grandmother died, leaving her in the care of her then seventy-six-year-old grandfather, Gabriel Sylliboy. The first elected Chief of the Mi'kmaw Grand Council, Gabriel never learned English, and insisted Murdena earn an English education worthy of her Mi'kmaw pride.

Sixty miles away, Albert Marshall was being homeschooled. His classroom, he explains, was the great outdoors; his teachers were his parents and the Elders of Eskasoni.

"They would transfer this knowledge to the younger ones, of how to appreciate and how to learn from nature," said Albert. "Why should I cut down this tree just for the sake of it? Why should I shoot that bird just for the sake of it? Because that bird has a purpose, just like I have a purpose."

Despite his early education, at the age of ten, Albert was sent to "a prison called Shubenacadie Residential School," where he was taught "just the opposite."

"During those years...they did everything to eradicate the spirit of who I am as a Mi'kmaw. But they could never touch my spirit. In my spirit was the spirit of my language," said Albert, who retained his language throughout. "I have to say, I was very fortunate."

Meanwhile Murdena did her own time at "another prison" called the St. Joseph's Residential Convent, a predominantly non-Native school for girls.

Dropping out her final year, Murdena met Albert, and let's say, things started looking up for these two L'nu'k. Together they left for Massachusetts to work "anywhere" that was hiring, eventually returning to Eskasoni, where they married in 1960, raising six children in rapid succession.

And so, the Marshall family flourished, until 1978 when their middle child, Tommy, then just fourteen years old, died of cancer. His death changed the course of Murdena and Albert's lives. The autopsy showed the cancer was triggered by a chemical called Agent Orange.

"That's when I decided I want to spend my full time trying to talk about and trying to protect Mother Earth," Albert said. He would travel to Europe and Vietnam to give talks on the dangers of Agent Orange, a chemical used to kill plants.

After the trauma, Murdena also became determined to help preserve the language and culture of her people. She enrolled and soon graduated from Truro's teacher's college and, in 1984, graduated with a bachelor of education from the University of New Brunswick. The moment she learned she'd been accepted to study her master's in the States, she turned to Albert and said: "Looks like we better pack up Nick the dog: we're going to Harvard."

After earning her master's there, they returned to Eskasoni, where Murdena was soon hired by Cape Breton University (CBU). According to CBU, her vision, along with that of other Mi'kmaw contemporaries like Alexander Denny, was important in shaping present-day Unama'ki College. Meanwhile, Murdena was becoming increasingly worried at how few Indigenous students she spotted on campus. She and Arthur decided to bring their concerns to community Elders. The Elders in turn explained the only way Indigenous youth would want to be part of the system that had colonized their culture would be if these same schools included Indigenous knowledge systems. After much discussion, Albert eventually created the term *Etuaptmumk*, or "Two-Eyed Seeing." Etuaptmumk includes the idea that all ways of knowing have equal value. So, rather than assume "one" Indigenous or "one" Western way of being, doing, and thinking is superior to all others, Etuaptmumk encourages educators to integrate all ways of knowing into teaching and learning.

Etuaptmumk was a ground-breaking term. After introducing the idea in the 1990s, Elders Albert and Murdena created the Integrative Science program at Cape Breton University, which ran for almost twenty years, and included Mi'kmaw and Western knowledge.

And while Murdena remained active well into her retirement, the beloved Elder, professor, wife, mother, and great-grandmother left us for the Spirit World in 2018. Murdena and Albert were married fifty-eight years.

EXAMPLE OF ETUAPTMUMK

A simple example of Etuaptmumk could be learning from your grandmother that a plant like mint is good to eat when you're feeling sick (one way of knowing), then learning in a science class that certain chemical compounds in mint leaf help to settle your stomach (another way). And finally, after noticing that your stomach gets upset whenever you eat something with a lot of milk in it, like ice cream, learning to change your diet. (Ta-da: yet another way of knowing.) All these ways of knowing are helpful, and when you combine them, your knowledge becomes richer and deeper. (And your stomach feels better.)

"She did leave quite a legacy. She was known globally, because of her teaching and storytelling ability. The legacy that she has created is very, very much impossible for us to live up to," Albert said.

But Albert has never stopped trying.

A razor-sharp thinker well into his eighties, Albert continues to share their combined vision, delivering lectures on Integrative Science and Etuaptmumk. And their hard work is paying off. In the spring of 2022, Nova Scotia's Department of Education and Early Childhood Development announced plans to launch a Two-Eyed Seeing pilot program in high schools across the province.

SELECT AWARDS, HONOURS & PUBLICATIONS

JOINT

❋ Recipients, Honorary Doctor of Letters, Cape Breton University (CBU), 2009

ALBERT MARSHALL

❋ Marshall Award for Aboriginal Leadership, Eco-Hero Awards, Nova Scotia Environmental Network, 2009

MURDENA MARSHALL

❋ *Muin and the Seven Bear Hunters: A Mi'kmaw Night Sky Story/Muin aqq L'uiknek Te'sijik Ntuksuinu'k: Mi'kmawey Tepkikewey Musikiskey A'tukwaqn*, Cape Breton University Press, 2010

❋ Grand Chief Donald Marshall Senior Memorial Elder Award, Premier Rodney MacDonald, Government of Nova Scotia, 2006

❋ National Aboriginal Role Model Award, Eskasoni First Nation, 1996

❋ Outstanding Leadership Award, Eskasoni First Nation, 1989

ELDER MARILYN SARK
A LEAKY ROOF TO A BROKEN TOE

Born: March 23, 1942
Lennox Island First Nation, PEI

"Because we were almost a mile off the coast, people made the trip to the doctor only when they were really sick," said Marilyn Sark, the first Epekwitnewaq Mi'kmaw to earn a nursing degree. "Many women had to have their babies at home. We had no health services of our own."

Before the ocean froze over, a fishing boat was used to ferry the few hundred Mi'kmaw residents on and off Lennox Island, where she grew up. In the winters, people were forced to cross on the ice either by foot or by horse and sleigh.

"I can remember people helping a mother bring her sick child across the ice to Port Hill, pulling a hand sleigh covered in cardboard to shelter the child," she said. "Once across they also needed a drive to the hospital. There were no cars on Lennox Island. So there were quite a lot of harrowing experiences at that time."

Marilyn—a practicing nurse in Charlottetown and Alberton since 1963—her husband, Jack Sark, and their four children returned to Lennox Island in 1972. That same year Jack became Chief of Lennox Island, and Marilyn set up her nursing practice in a small ground-floor apartment near the general store. Only in 1973 was a bridge built connecting Lennox Island to the rest of PEI.

"I wasn't called out every night, you know, but I knew I could be. With four young boys at home, it could get stressful."

While a local doctor from Tyne Valley crossed the bridge to put in a few clinic hours a week, the rest all fell to Marilyn. "I used to say anything 'from a leaky roof to a broken toe'—everything came by me. I was on call 24/7 because I was also the half-time welfare officer."

From coordinating Alcoholics Anonymous meetings and dental appointments to providing transportation so patients could see specialists, Marilyn served her community for twenty years. Even after a dedicated health centre was constructed in 1990, Marilyn remained the only full-time, on-site health-care specialist until 1992, when she left to become president of the Aboriginal Nurses Association of Canada (ANAC).

After serving as ANAC's president for two terms she went back to nursing on Lennox Island. Well into her late seventies, she continues to coordinate child development teams at the Lennox Island Health Centre and the Abegweit Health Centre, and maintain shifts helping people detox at health centres in Summerside and Alberton.

She plans to slow down after her eightieth birthday. "Then it's time to pull away and let somebody else take over."

When asked how she feels about her distinguished career, she remained humble and matter of fact: "I just did whatever was in front of me and needed to be done. I just did my job the same as most people do."

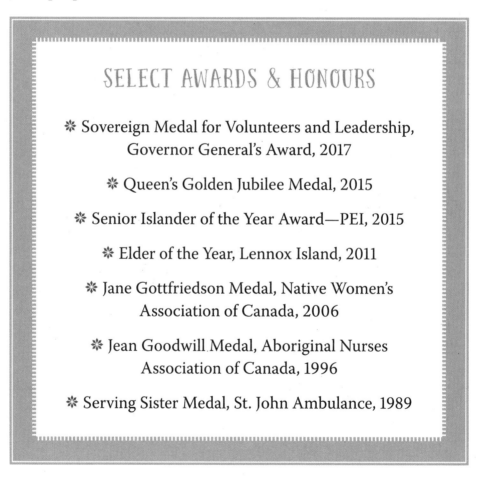

SELECT AWARDS & HONOURS

✤ Sovereign Medal for Volunteers and Leadership, Governor General's Award, 2017

✤ Queen's Golden Jubilee Medal, 2015

✤ Senior Islander of the Year Award—PEI, 2015

✤ Elder of the Year, Lennox Island, 2011

✤ Jane Gottfriedson Medal, Native Women's Association of Canada, 2006

✤ Jean Goodwill Medal, Aboriginal Nurses Association of Canada, 1996

✤ Serving Sister Medal, St. John Ambulance, 1989

CHRIS GOOGOO
AN ASTRONAUT AND A FEATHER

Born: December 27, 1972
We'koqma'q First Nation, NS

"We try to light the embers of creativity and imaginations for these kids," said Chris Googoo, chief operating officer of Ulnooweg Education Centre's Science & Innovation Program (formerly Digital Mi'kmaq), which aims to bring science, technology, engineering, and math (STEM) to more Indigenous youth.

The son of Raymond and Annie Isabel (née Bernard) Googoo, Christopher grew up surrounded by community serving L'nu'k. "My dad was a councillor; my uncles were Chiefs. So I was right there, always hearing [about] the importance of community and actually helping people." He adds his love of learning, nurtured by both parents and one science teacher, started young. "We had a wonderful teacher, Andy Sarka. I think he wanted to make sure that we were learning properly in those years. He remained with us from Grades 7 to 9 as a group."

Following high school, Chris went to St. Francis Xavier University, where he earned a bachelor of business administration degree. He also began working with Ulnooweg, an innovative not-for-profit organization dedicated to the success of Indigenous communities, individuals, and businesses. Within seven years he was promoted to general manager, and by 2017, became Ulnooweg's chief operating officer. A year later, he launched an innovative education program at Ulnooweg, Digital Mi'kmaq. Digital Mi'kmaq is now known as Science & Innovation, to be more inclusive. Focused on Etuaptmumk as well as Netukulimk, Science & Innovation is driven to inspire Indigenous children to pursue more STEM-based learning.

"And when we do that, of course, we want the best of the best," he said.

Since 2018, Science & Innovation has forged partnerships with the Canadian Space Agency, Dalhousie University's Institute for Big Data Analytics, and Montreal's artificial intelligence agency Mila. He says even the Canadian Research Chair in Big Data Analytics for Digital Agriculture, Stan Matwin, came on board to teach young children about big data personally.

Meanwhile Chris says these Indigenous ways of knowing—the interconnectedness of all life and the integration of multiple ways of seeing—are important to everyone's futures.

"So when our Elders tell us to go into the forest and hug trees, there's actually science behind that interconnectedness. Like the fungus and mycelium or 'wood-wide web' underneath talks to the whole forest and the plants around it," Chris said. "This is what our Elders always said. And when this validation occurs and is accepted on both sides, then I think you have true reconciliation."

In 2021 Ulnooweg also launched a Community Garden and Food Security project in five First Nation communities in Atlantic Canada. Prior to this project, finding decent fresh produce meant L'nu'k from these communities had to travel up to fifty-five kilometres. Now they have a food centre on site. That same year the organization also acquired Windhorse Farms, a two-hundred-acre plot of ancient forests based in Lunenburg County, NS, as a new education and healing facility.

From online spaces to schoolrooms and ancient forests, Digital Mi'kmaq even left the mark of the Mi'kmaq on the final frontier when Canadian astronaut David Saint-Jacques blasted into space in late 2018. Thanks to Chris Googoo and L'nuey children, who fondly dubbed the astronaut *Ta'pit* ("David" in Mi'kmaw), the astronaut brought some symbolic Mi'kmaw items on his ride to the International Space Station: an eagle feather and a miniature handmade basket.

"It makes me believe that anything is possible," said Shanna Francis, the woman who wove the basket to be no larger than a loonie. "I hope it might in some way open new doors for the youth in our community."

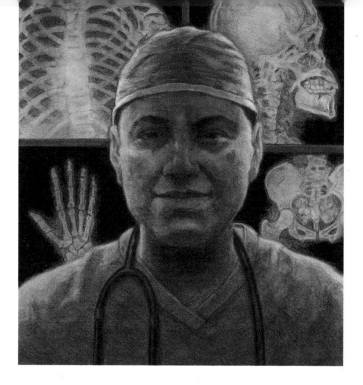

DR. ROB JOHNSON
A PHYSICIAN'S PERSPECTIVE

Born: July 16, 1973
Millbrook First Nation, NS

The son of Robert Johnson Senior and Shirley Francis, Dr. Rob Johnson said his family encouraged him to respect multiple perspectives.

"Growing up in the seventies and eighties, it seemed like everybody was family," said Rob. "And that allowed me the freedom to not only befriend and learn from others, but also to respect the differences of others. And I think that was probably my most important learning."

The first Mi'kmaw to ever earn a medical degree, Rob said he began dreaming of becoming a doctor in Grade 5.

"I had to basically make a presentation to my classmates about the layers of the skin. And it was quite detailed," he said. "From that point on, it was always in the back of my mind. Almost every day I wanted to do very well in school." Every year to follow, Rob managed to do at least one school project on human anatomy.

And while his passion for science was rooted in his studies, he said sports helped him gain the discipline he needed to excel. In high school Robert played provincial AAA hockey as a forward.

"Sport helped me learn how to be disciplined and contribute to a team, which has carried over into my professional life," he said. "I'm also a believer that the mind works best when you have a certain level of physical fitness."

Despite his athletic skills, his older cousin recalled Rob's commitment to medicine from a young age.

"I remember I said, 'Why don't you keep pushing on? Because you could continue to play,' and Rob said, 'No, I have to re-evaluate and set my priorities and focus on what's realistic,'" Chief Bob Gloade told the *Dalhousie News*. "For someone seventeen years old, to know what he wanted and what he was committed to was significant. He is respected in the community for his ability to do that and for his accomplishments."

After high school Rob earned a bachelor of science and went on to study medicine at Dalhousie University. While at school he served as president of the Aboriginal Student Association. He also became the Aboriginal delegate for both the Canadian Federation of Students and the Student Union of Nova Scotia, while serving on Dal's Minorities in Medicine Committee. He won the National Aboriginal Achievement Award (Youth) from Indspire in 1996 and in his youth won over twenty scholarships and awards for both athletics and academics.

Before receiving his medical degree in 1998, he even took time to study traditional herbal medicines and volunteer at a local soup kitchen.

Keen to explore the world, Rob went to BC after graduation to study emergency medicine and anesthesiology, where he met his wife—another doctor and a member of the Carrier-Tsilhqot'in First Nation. The two settled down and began a family.

A father of three and role model to many, Rob wholeheartedly advocates for careers in STEM while also respecting the inclusion of multiple perspectives.

"Growing up in a First Nation community and practicing medicine are both tremendous honours. That combination molded me into a physician who gives the best possible care to each individual, while highly respecting the story behind each. I know first-hand what obstacles the Indigenous peoples have been born into. I was there, and to some extent I always will be."

DID YOU KNOW?
THE MEDICINE WHEEL
& THE FOUR DIRECTIONS

An important Mi'kmaw symbol, the Medicine Wheel is known to represent the four elements as well as the four directions. In addition, it symbolizes important Indigenous principles alongside the cycles of life.
To follow is just one such interpretation, offered by Epekwitk Elder Keptin John Joe Sark.
***East** is yellow like the rising sun, representing the place of all new beginnings.*
***South** is black and represents adulthood, the stage where people acquire the things needed for life, like wisdom and self-forgiveness.*
***West** is red and represents healing, the place of returning to the Creator, a higher spiritual plane than the beginning.*
***North** is white like snow, representing Elders and the respect owed to them, and also the importance of youth and Elders coming together to help each other.*
You can see a medicine wheel depicted on the cover of this book.

JENNIFER SYLLIBOY
SWEETGRASS SOLUTIONS

Born: April 1983

Eskasoni First Nation, NS

"Every summer my grandmother would take me sweetgrass picking. We would jump in the car, and she would drive me out to these meadows and just big old fields where sweetgrass was growing," Jennifer Sylliboy said of Murdena Marshall. "She taught me how to identify it by the colouring of the roots, how to pick it, and how to ensure that it continues to grow."

The daughter of Joanne (née Lewis) and Jerry Marshall, Jennifer says her grandparents, Albert and Murdena Marshall, "lived and breathed" Etuaptmumk and Netukulimk, adding that her grandmother taught her how to use plants in traditional ways.

"Growing up, almost every year I had different ideas of what I wanted to be. One year I wanted to be a doctor, the next, an RCMP officer, then a forensic scientist. Like, there's a whole bunch of stuff I wanted to do over the years," she said, laughing.

Despite being good at science and math as a kid, Jennifer said she only connected it to Etuaptmumk, or being an Indigenous Two-Eyed Seer, much later.

"It was so natural to me, I just did it all the time. And because I went through the whole education system, it was never really encouraged. People never really found these other ways of knowing to be as credible as Western science."

After completing high school in Truro, Jennifer returned to Cape Breton to enroll in Cape Breton University's (CBU) bachelor of science program. A few years after becoming the proud mother to Sali'j, Jennifer and her daughter left for Calgary, where she earned her master's degree in science and settled down to work...only to pick up and leave the moment she learned her grandmother was ill.

"I realized I needed to spend the rest of her days with her back in Eskasoni. So I packed up my daughter and we drove across the country."

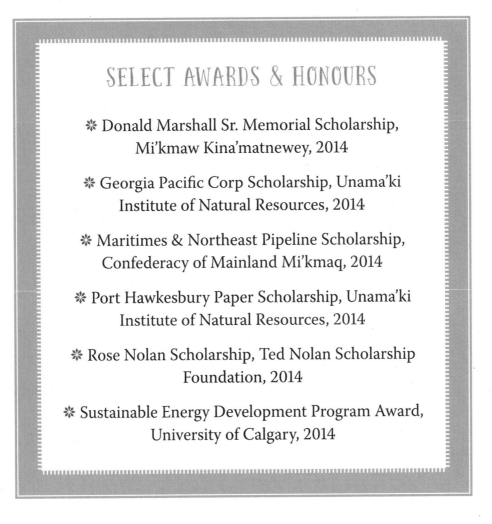

SELECT AWARDS & HONOURS

✤ Donald Marshall Sr. Memorial Scholarship, Mi'kmaw Kina'matnewey, 2014

✤ Georgia Pacific Corp Scholarship, Unama'ki Institute of Natural Resources, 2014

✤ Maritimes & Northeast Pipeline Scholarship, Confederacy of Mainland Mi'kmaq, 2014

✤ Port Hawkesbury Paper Scholarship, Unama'ki Institute of Natural Resources, 2014

✤ Rose Nolan Scholarship, Ted Nolan Scholarship Foundation, 2014

✤ Sustainable Energy Development Program Award, University of Calgary, 2014

Back home in Cape Breton, Jennifer began work as an Integrative Knowledge Systems Researcher with the Unama'ki Institute of Natural Resources (UINR). As part of her role there she said she spoke "for many species with no voice," and strived "to help First Nation communities become stewards of their own lands and resources." In 2022, Jennifer moved across the country to work for Two Worlds Consulting as a Land and Culture Specialist. In this new job, she continues to help First Nation communities.

In particular, she hopes to prevent any more aquatic extinction events, noting Netukulimk teaches us that all living things are interconnected.

"We can't just worry about the salmon. We have to worry about the rivers, the oceans, the trees; everything connects together. As Mi'kmaw people, we are taught that everything is relationship-based. Everything is connected."

Jennifer encourages other L'nu'k to apply Two-Eyed Seeing in their own lives as well.

"It will actually give you an advantage later on. You'll be able to see things in a different way. And who knows, maybe you'll even create solutions that others have been struggling to find forever."

JORDAN ALEXANDER
SKATEBOARDS AND ROBOT FISH

Born: 1992
Qalipu First Nation, NL

E very summer, Jordan Alexander and his friends made a little bridge out of rocks to cross the brook running beside his parents' backyard. And every year, they got soaked trying to cross it.

He was ten when he finally figured it out.

"I remember realizing slowly that, unless we built it up extremely high, or filled in all the cracks, the water was just going to keep going over the rocks," said Jordan. "That was one of the many times I got intrigued by nature and wanted to learn how to work with it, instead of fighting against it."

Challenges like that led Jordan to study physics, and eventually, to master all sciences. The son of Tony and Karen Alexander of Stephenville, Newfoundland and Labrador, Jordan Alexander is a founding member of Qalipu First Nation and a Mechanical Engineer (EIT).

"That's kind of like why I went into mechanical engineering, because I was able to do whatever I wanted—like make, build, and design whatever. There's so much opportunity to be creative—to make something and actually bring it out into the world."

Before completing his engineering degree at Dalhousie, Jordan taught himself 3D modelling and design, and said he's been having fun with it ever since. An avid skateboarder and surfer, Jordan's already printed a truck base for his skateboard and new fins for his surfboard. Meanwhile Jordan said a career highlight so far has been collaborating with then eleven-year-old Jayla, another Mi'kmaw from We'koqma'q First Nation, on the Little Inventors' Challenge.

Based in the United Kingdom, Little Inventors is a creative education organization that turns "the practical to the fantastical" by pairing children's ideas and creating solutions with trained engineers and designers. According to Jordan, about a thousand kids submitted innovative ideas on how to better clean and protect the world's oceans. Of those, only about a hundred were selected to be trialled, and Jayla's was one. Given water-protecting has been a way of life in Mi'kma'ki for thousands of years, Jayla's idea was a natural selection, and Jordan was soon on board to be her mentor.

"I was seeing a lot of meaning, like proof that something was kind of ingrained in her or something. Like the colours she chose, for example—they were primarily all colours of the Mi'kmaw Medicine Wheel."

Jayla's idea was to make a "robot fish" out of biodegradable materials and program it to scour the ocean floor for manmade debris. Once its belly was full, the robot fish would surface, unload, and dive back down for more.

"Her concept drawing was at such a high level that I'm not sure she was even aware of it. Like the 'design by nature' aspect, for example, and the colourways," Jordan said. "Even just the art style... it was really cool."

As a mechanical engineer, the challenge for Jordan was use modern technology, in this case a 3D printer, to bring Jayla's robot fish to life, all in a sustainable and eco-friendly way. True to Jayla's vision, Jordan incorporated a design that uses PLA, a bioplastic made from corn and infused with a filler made of powdered scallop shells. When all was said and done, Little Inventors featured just eleven designs from around the world for their online exhibit, and Jayla's made the cut.

Since then, Jordan has returned to Stephenville, NL, and even started using his new 3D-printed fins to get in some winter surfing around St. George's Bay. And while he admits the waters of the Gulf of St. Lawrence are "definitely chilly," he's sure proud to have helped Jayla protect them.

"It's truly pretty amazing what you can do with science."

AARON PROSPER
A MIRACLE IN A PRINGLES JAR

Born: March 15, 1996
Eskasoni First Nation, NS

The son of Floyd and Dawna Prosper of Eskasoni First Nation, Aaron Prosper said he grew up immersed in the ways of Etuaptmumk. "The culture I was raised in, it was always encouraged to be curious and ask questions—which is great because that's kind of the basis of science."

Aaron's aptitude in Etuaptmumk has helped him succeed from the start. His curiosity led him to explore why Mi'kmaw communities have higher rates of diabetes. Using it as a high school science fair topic, he ended up entering the Canada Wide Science Fair (CWSF)/Expo-sciences pancanadienne (ESPC), winning bronze medals in his divisions two years in a row.

"That was kind of the first light-bulb moment," said Aaron. "The idea that you can create a project and get answers to the questions you had, while also learning cool things along the way."

Ready to get more answers to his questions, Aaron left the reserve to attend Dalhousie University in 2014. Nonetheless, he made sure to pack some "cool things" to bring along with him. Tucked away in his boxes was one of his most prized possessions: his family **Waltes** set. A traditional Mi'kmaw dice-and-bowl game, it was so much fun it was said to be "favoured by the Spirit World." This fun scared the Canadian government so much that, until the 1960s, it was illegal for L'nu'k to play it. Elders across Eskasoni had

SELECT AWARDS, HONOURS & PUBLICATIONS

❋ Kausattumi Scholarship, Atlantic Indigenous Mentorship Awards, 2019

❋ President, Dalhousie Student Union, 2018–2019

❋ Top DSU Council Member, Dalhousie Student IMPACT Awards, 2017

❋ Bronze Medal Excellence Award, Senior, Canada Wide Science Fair, 2014

❋ Bronze Medal Excellence Award, Senior, Canada Wide Science Fair, 2013

hidden their sets away, and Aaron's grandparents taught him how to play as a child.

"It's not like I can pack up a sweat lodge and bring it with me to the city," he said, laughing. "My grandfather actually wrote all the rules on a piece of loose leaf and tucked them away in a Pringles jar."

While at Dalhousie, Aaron served as the Indigenous student representative and, by 2018, was elected president of the Dalhousie Student Union.

"I had a lot of support from other Indigenous students at the time," he said. After completing his bachelor's in neuroscience,

Aaron went on to study his master's in applied health research and picked up work with the Union of Nova Scotia Mi'kmaq. In 2021, Aaron was hired as Nova Scotia Health's Indigenous health consultant, where his job is to help Indigenous folks better understand and access the province's health-care programs. For example, for those Mi'kmaq who speak English as a second language, the COVID-19 pandemic initially created some confusion. Some Elders expressed concerns that beavers in their area were spreading a terrible disease, given the Mi'kmaw word for beaver—**kopit**—is pronounced "go-bit," which sounds like "covid."

Thanks to his skills in Etuaptmumk as well as his skills as a leader, Aaron's future is wide open, and in all the four directions.

DID YOU KNOW?

Traditionally L'nu'k sought and harvested physical and spiritual medicine from the lush forests, riverbanks, and meadows of Mi'kma'ki. For example, smudging, a spiritual cleansing technique, takes place when common herbs like sweetgrass, sage, tobacco, and cedar are burned. It's believed that, as the herbs are released into the flame, the ensuing smoke wraps around negative energy and whisks it away for good. Generations of L'nu'k have also used everything from the roots of goldthread to the twigs of juniper trees, the sap of the white spruce to the bark of cherry trees to master remedies for such common health ailments as the flu, mouth sores, and even bladder infections.

When he's not working on his studies or job, Aaron enjoys drumming with the Eastern Eagle Singers, a Mi'kmaw contemporary powwow drum group, and the band Alan Syliboy and the Thundermakers. Nearly a decade after providing his first Waltes workshops, Aaron continues to share his love of the game and his grandpa's rules to this day.

PART VI

CRUSADERS & ENTREPRENEURS

"I encourage all First Nations peoples and governments to step up to the plate and demand their piece of the pie. Our success lies in building on the innovations of today while at the same time, incorporating Indigenous knowledge based on the principles of conservation, sustainability of resources, and reverence for the lands and the waters."

–Business Leader and Corporate Lawyer **Bernd Christmas**, Membertou First Nation

"Indigenous designers...we haven't been given the opportunity to show the world fully yet what our art is capable of."

–Entrepreneur and Bead Artist **Cheyenne Isaac-Gloade**, Listuguj First Nation

"At the end of the day, it's really about common sense. Focusing on solutions as opposed to working on the problems. Problems are always more expensive than solutions."

–Entrepreneur and Leader **Jenene Wooldridge**, Abegweit First Nation

ELDER DOREEN JENKINS
A STRONG MI'KMAW WOMAN

Born: May 1, 1952

Lennox Island First Nation, PEI

Long before entrepreneur and Elder Doreen (née Francis) Jenkins became a grandmother to fifteen, mother to eight, and inspiration to many, she was just another kid running underfoot. While Doreen was still a young girl, her parents Bertha and Arthur Francis packed her, her seven siblings, and all their Lennox Island belongings, and headed for the United States in search of work.

Eventually settling in New Hampshire at nine years old, Doreen said she was hopeful after her first day in an American public school. "The teacher was so kind. She said to the other children, 'This is an Indian girl from a small province in Canada called Prince Edward Island,' and the kids were so excited to ask me questions."

Glowing from the attention, Doreen was excited to return the next day. "I dressed very carefully to make sure I would be presentable and everything, I was so happy to go to school." When she arrived, however, a mob of Grade 8 kids gathered around her and began kicking her. "Because I was Native, you see, I had the daylights kicked out of me and landed in [hospital]. After that, I was just walking with my head held down, don't talk to anybody."

Resolved to quietly make her way, Doreen finished high school and enrolled at Michael's Hair Design. Graduating from their two-year program in 1975, she returned to PEI, where she worked as a hairdresser, then as a barber, for the next fifty years.

"I think barbering appealed to me because it focused on a different strength—to be able to face my fears of working around men and to speak up and have my voice," Doreen said, whose business, Doreen's Barber Shop, bustled on Charlottetown's North River Road for many years.

And while she enjoyed barbering, she closed shop a few years ago, opting to cut for just a few loyal clients from her home, a farm in Canoe Cove, PEI. Otherwise, the respected Elder divides her time between First Nations consulting—helping everyone from the local RCMP to elementary school children, university students to government employees—and running the Living Nativity and Light Show, an annual fundraising event she conceived with her husband.

Every year since 2010, Doreen and her husband, Chrys, have transformed their home on PEI's south shore into a holiday spectacle. A highly anticipated annual outing for many PEI families featuring a stunning display of holiday lighting, the Living Nativity and Light Show showcases a manger scene replete with actors playing Mary, Joseph, the Three Wise Men, an assortment of shepherds and angels, real farm animals, and live choir performances to boot. What's more, Santa and Mrs. Claus have been known to drop by unannounced on an old-fashioned sleigh. All of Chrys and Doreen's proceeds are donated to local charity every year.

"I am blessed to have a loving and supportive husband and family, and we all enjoy doing our part in order to support the greater good."

A role model to many, Elder Doreen is a great example of someone who's chosen to overcome life's obstacles and multiply joy for others.

"My trials and tribulations shaped me into the strong woman I am today, and I'm so grateful."

SENETL DAN CHRISTMAS
THE FLOWERING TREE

Born: September 10, 1956
Membertou First Nation, NS

As the eldest of six born to Viola and Augustus Christmas, one might say Dan Christmas was born to lead. His grandfather, the late Chief Ben Christmas, was the president of both the United General Indian Council of Nova Scotia and the North American Indian Brotherhood. His tireless efforts to stop the Canadian government's plan to move all Indigenous people onto specific plots of land called "reserves"—something known as the "centralization policy"—helped to protect the Mi'kmaw culture for generations. Only ten when his grandfather died, Dan took after him.

"I remember he was always working—his office was always full of papers. And what I remember most about him is how well he treated everyone. He treated everyone with respect," Dan said. "He was a shining example of what a leader should be."

Though badly wounded in World War Two, Dan's father, Sma'knis Augustus Christmas, was appointed **Pu'tu's** by the Grand Council—an honourable role, given the Pu'tu's is responsible for negotiating and maintaining all agreements between Nations. Nineteen when his father died, Dan left university to begin working and help provide for his younger siblings. His mother, Viola, also returned to work. "She worked full-time while raising the six of us. We never went without."

A few years later Dan met and married the love of his life, Arlene "Dozay" Nicholas, a Wolastoqiyik artist from Tobique First Nation. He recalls her support when he committed to helping bring his community, Membertou First Nation, back from bankruptcy.

"My wife had given me a beautiful, big dream catcher. And in the middle was a piece of leather. And on it, she wrote, *Bring to life the flowering tree of your people*," he said. "I always took that as my personal mandate."

Dan's charismatic leadership would indeed ignite the passion of his people, uniting the community of Membertou to work as a team. And work they did. Under Dan's leadership, Membertou's workforce exploded to twenty times its original size, soon turning their economically bankrupt community into a wealthy one with tens of millions of dollars. It was Dan too who led the Mi'kmaw response to the Report of the Royal Commission on the Donald Marshall Junior Prosecution. Dan is also credited as the driving force behind the 1999 Supreme Court of Canada ruling that re-enforced the Mi'kmaw treaty right to trade fish.

In 2016 Dan was approached by other Mi'kmaw leaders to see if he'd be willing to attempt to become a Canadian Senator. While initially he wasn't sold on the idea, the former Assembly of First Nations regional Chief, Morley Googoo, knew exactly how to change his mind. "He asked me what I felt it would mean for our Nation's young people if a Mi'kmaw person was in Parliament, and that was it. He knew he had me then."

Sworn in that December, Dan became both the first Mi'kmaw person to serve in Canada's Senate as well as the first Senator to open a full-service office outside of Ottawa. On the day of his grand opening, well-wishers spilled out onto Membertou's sidewalks, and the office sign read: *Senetl Daniel Christmas: Senit W'jit Kanata*, or "Senator Daniel Christmas, Senate of Canada." Among his countless accomplishments as Senator, the passing of Bill C-15 in June 2021,

SELECT AWARDS & HONOURS

❊ Impact Award, Cape Breton Partnership, 2014

❊ Queen Elizabeth II Diamond Jubilee Medal, Governor General of Canada, 2012

❊ National Excellence in Aboriginal Leadership Award, Aboriginal Financial Officers Association, 2008

❊ Honorary Doctor of Laws, Dalhousie University, 2005

the United Nations Declaration on the Rights of Indigenous Peoples (UNDRIP), has been his proudest so far. With the passing of Bill C-15, Canada signalled that it stands among those Nations around the world willing to uphold the minimum standards for the survival, dignity, and well-being of Indigenous people.

And when he's not busy restoring justice and pride to Indigenous Canadians, Dan is home raising his youngest child. While his wife Arlene "Dozay" sadly left for the Spirit World in 2019, remarkable blossoms continue to bloom on the tree his grandfather planted and which she so lovingly nurtured.

JENENE WOOLDRIDGE
THE RED ISLAND'S LIGHT & HER LEADERS

Born: February 4, 1982
Abegweit First Nation, PEI

Even as a little girl, Jenene Wooldridge's first adventures as "an entrepreneur" reveal her deep connection to the land.

"We had so much fun living by the water. We would gather [up the red] clay and make small bowls and pots from it...I'd also paint seashells and set up a stand to sell [everything] at the end of the driveway," said Jenene.

Named one of the "Top 25 Most Powerful Women in Business" by *Atlantic Business Magazine* in 2021, Jenene came by her leadership skills naturally. Born and raised in Epekwitk,

LATERAL VIOLENCE

When people experience oppression, they often push down the feelings that arise because of it—feelings like anger, shame, and rage. Lateral violence happens when they take out their negative feelings on anyone else in a similarly powerless position (peers and relatives, for example), especially if that other person is succeeding at overcoming oppression and regaining their power. Lateral violence is a form of bullying, and it manifests as jealousy, resentment, blame, and bitterness towards those who are trying to get ahead.

Jenene is the daughter of former Chief James and Carolyn (née Francis), while her family's tradition of Epekwitk Chiefdom stretches back generations.

Meanwhile her first experiences with racism and "lateral violence" only occurred when she got older.

Unfettered, she said, "I made the decision that I was not going to let anyone or anything stop me from sharing my gifts with others. I'm confident in myself and that's what matters most." Jenene discovered she had a unique perspective as an Indigenous woman that would guide her through future work.

True to her word, Jenene focused her career on building others up—especially her Indigenous peers. Through her business **Segewa't** Consulting (*segewa't* means "to rise"), Jenene and her

Along with potatoes and Anne of Green Gables, *Epekwitk is famous for its red beaches and coastlines. But did you ever wonder how these red earth tones came to be? Well, it would seem this red hue has everything to do with the open air, iron, and a special little crystal, hematite. According to scientists, most of the Earth has spent ages submerged underwater. It's believed the Island, however, has remained above water just long enough to transform its sandstone into iron. Over time, more chemical reactions have occurred, coating this iron sandstone in tiny hematite crystals. And these hematite crystals are said to absorb all colours of light except the colour red.*

So, the next time someone talks about the Island's red clay, just remember the enduring little hematite crystal.

And, of course, the Mi'kmaq, who've lived there thousands of years, too.

team offer a range of specialized leadership training designed to support First Nation individuals and communities achieve their goals.

Determined to help other L'nu'k, Jenene spent more than a decade serving in a range of First Nation leadership positions before becoming L'nuey's executive director in 2019. L'nuey, which means "belonging to the people," is an initiative focused on protecting the rights of the Mi'kmaq of Epekwitk. Jenene is their first executive director.

"Being a leader includes being respectful, decisive, and inclusive. It's a way of being," Jenene said. "When you live with intention, you know your purpose, your strengths, and you are able to live more fully."

Inspired by Medicine Wheel teachings, Jenene also became an author in 2021. Published by Acorn Press, the *Living Full Circle Planner* is a weekly undated planner that focuses on encouraging others to lead their lives with intention and balance.

And in 2023, Jenene was the recipient of the Queen's Platinum Jubilee Medal for her significant contributions as a Mi'kmaw leader and ongoing efforts to promote truth and reconciliation across Epekwitk.

BERND CHRISTMAS
FROM THE HEART PERSPECTIVE
Membertou First Nation, NS

While he was born in Membertou, by the time Bernd Christmas was a teen, he'd already lived all over the world. That's because his dad was a member of the armed forces, and, like all military families, the Christmas family was required to relocate every couple of years. So when Bernd started thinking about options after high school, his sights were already set on the big world beyond. That's probably why he asked his dad whether he, too, should consider a future in the armed forces.

As Bernd remembers, his father scoffed. "'In the armed forces, you have to be able to take orders," Bernd said, recollecting his father with a laugh. "'You're a guy that doesn't take orders. No one will ever be able to tell you what to do. You'll need to blaze your own trail.'"

And as it turns out, that's exactly what he did. After graduating from Osgoode Hall Law School, Bernd became the first ever Mi'kmaw lawyer, setting up a lucrative practice in Toronto, Ontario, with a Bay Street law firm.

Nonetheless, his parents eventually settled back in Membertou. Perhaps this is why, at Membertou Chief Terrance Paul's request, Bernd abandoned his successful Bay Street career in 1995 to assume the role of Membertou's chief executive officer. Alongside Chief Paul, Bernd recruited Dan Christmas, and the three created a set of processes that helped stop their community from becoming bankrupt. In particular, Bernd was key in Membertou getting

International Organization for Standardization (ISO) certification in 2002, making it the first Indigenous government in the world to do so. With ISO certification, Membertou signalled to the global community that their community's processes and systems were in line with the highest standards of quality and safety in the world.

As Bernd explains, when a First Nation becomes ISO certified, "It means that everyone [within the First Nation] knows exactly what they need to do in order to work together towards achieving the same goal." Membertou's ISO certification means that their Chief, Council, and other members of management all promise to follow the same goals for sustainability, conservation, innovation, and success.

By 2006, Membertou had gone from being a First Nation government that owed a million dollars to one with several million in the bank. Since helping his home community of Membertou, Bernd has volunteered a lot of time and energy to help other First Nations do the same.

"Trillions of dollars are traded in the world economy each day," Bernd said. "I encourage all First Nations peoples and governments to step up to the plate and demand their piece of the pie."

Though Bernd is far from the first Mi'kmaw businessperson to encounter prejudice, the internationally renowned CEO and corporate lawyer is still forced to face down some damaging stereotypes. "There are some out of naiveté who might say, you know, that just because I am wearing a white shirt, tie, and suit, and not wearing regalia, 'You're not like the rest of them. Why's that?'" Bernd said. "And dealing with that level of overt racism happened a lot. And that's a tough position to be in because you're trying to counteract that. So, it's always about finding balances. You have to stop yourself from living up to the expectation of what others want you to be."

Striving to live up to his own expectations, Bernd uses his influence to instead forge profitable relationships between the corporate world and Indigenous communities. "There are lots of other circumstances I was very happy to be an agent of change," Bernd said, adding that he often encouraged Netukulimk-focused businesses to partner with local Indigenous communities.

Bernd's proudest achievements so far are his own children.

"With my children, I try to show, rather than tell. Like bring them to the community, to Membertou, and show them what it's like. As opposed to, you know, telling them. I also try to expose them to others that might help them on their paths."

After noticing how much his youngest, Ansale'wit, loved horses, Bernd took her to ride a pony at the fair, and by age four, she was already making national headlines in adult equestrian (horse riding) competitions. Bernd has travelled with his son Mykeo to college campuses across the United States to check out their soccer facilities firsthand, and introduced his oldest, Kai, a musician currently performing in the Montreal-based electronica band Of the Veil, to other established musicians.

"My words of wisdom for young readers would be, just keep moving ahead and think big, regardless of what people keep telling you. If you keep doing what you love, you'll wind up being successful. For sure from your own heart perspective, but then ultimately, others will recognize your talent, too."

MARY BETH DOUCETTE
THE REFRESHING RISE OF
INDIGENOUS BUSINESS

Born: December 1980
Membertou First Nation, NS

"**M**y dad always told me you need to take responsibility and learn to do things for yourself. Nobody is going to do anything for you," Mary Beth Doucette said.

The daughter of schoolteachers Frank and Theresa Doucette, Mary Beth said her parents always urged her to get involved in her community.

"I think those types of activities [...] help you learn you can make a difference. That you can go out in the community and make positive changes."

Excelling at school, Mary Beth went to Dalhousie to become an industrial engineer. After earning her degree in 2004, she moved to Ontario for work. Missing home terribly, she was afraid to return—she was concerned she'd never find work.

"So, I decided if I want to live and work in Nova Scotia, I need to learn how to create more jobs."

In 2006, Mary Beth packed up and moved home, enrolling at Cape Breton University (CBU) to learn exactly how to create work. Keen to learn how Membertou First Nation turned its economy around while keeping Mi'kmaw culture at the forefront, she began working with and learning from key members of Membertou's community. By 2011, the folks at CBU were so impressed with her community work that she was appointed Associate to the Purdy Crawford Chair, which means she was promoted to help support research into Indigenous business practices for the university. Over the next few years, Mary Beth co-wrote and edited *Indigenous Business in Canada: Principles and Practices* with colleagues Keith Brown and Janice Tulk. Published in 2016, the book is considered a must-read for anyone interested in studying Indigenous business. Promoted from the Associate Chair to the full-time position of Purdy Crawford Chair in 2018, Mary Beth now devotes all her time to researching Indigenous business practices, whether through her own doctoral studies or through teaching university students about Indigenous businesses models across Canada.

Mary Beth explained what an Indigenous business model can be, and how Etuaptmumk might be applied to, say, kids hoping to sell lemonade on a local street corner:

"Well first of all, even though it's called *Two*-Eyed Seeing, the concept is really about seeing *multiple* perspectives. So then, from a Two-Eyed Seeing perspective, the lemonade stand could offer multiple options for different types of cups to drink from. So, Styrofoam could be one option, since it's cheaper, but also paper cups, since they're better for the environment. They may even want to suggest customers bring their own cups to reuse," she said. "The other piece is there could be multiple options for the drink itself. And since lemons don't grow locally, more sustainable choices than lemonade could be juices made from locally sourced apples, rhubarb, cranberries, and blueberries, for example."

And while her work focuses on the Indigenous business model, especially those businesses that apply Etuaptmumk, she said it's important these aspiring entrepreneurs are aware of their own options, too. "Whether or not we want to be part of the Canadian economy, we need to know the rules that guide it. And if we don't want to be, well that's okay too. But we have to first understand the rules to know what our choices are."

SELECT AWARDS, HONOURS & PUBLICATIONS

✻ Judge, We'koqma'q Mi'kmaw School's Mi'kmaw Regional Science Fair, 2019

✻ Co-host, Music Mogul Event, Shannon School of Business Entrepreneurship Week, 2018

✻ Co-Editor, *Indigenous Business in Canada: Principles and Practices*, 2016

✻ Vital Award, Cape Breton Excellence Awards, 2015

SAVVY SIMON
UNLIMITED LOVE TO GIVE

Elsipogtog First Nation, NB

A well-known motivational speaker, entrepreneur, and activist, Savannah "Savvy" Simon was raised by her mother, Heidi Simon, and grandmother, Sarah Simon. Among the oldest of a huge group of cousins and the eldest of three siblings, Savvy was counted on to lend a hand to her mother and "Migi" (short for "**Migitjo**," which means grandmother in the Mi'kmaw Listuguj orthography). A born leader and entertainer, Savvy often thanks the influence of the strong women she grew up with. Most of all, she says her Migi (a residential school survivor) taught her to value grace, forgiveness and the importance of nurturing children early on.

After finishing high school, Savvy earned a business diploma and quickly landed a government job with benefits. And while she appreciated the security of a desk job, she says her spirit wasn't happy, so she continued with her passions on the side.

A fancy shawl powwow dancer, she auditioned and was selected to perform for the opening ceremonies at Vancouver's Olympics in 2010. In 2012, she became the first Indigenous woman to perform at Dollywood, the theme park of country singer Dolly Parton. The next year Savvy stood as a prayer warrior with Elsipogtog First Nation in her community's No Fracking blockade. She was also hired by Mi'kmaw Kina'matnewey to coordinate the Red Road Project. This project led Mi'kmaw youth away from peer pressure by educating them on the dangers of substance abuse and provided a supportive atmosphere to learn about Mi'kmaw culture by speaking Mi'kmaw and learning from Elders.

Quickly noticing a huge demand for Mi'kmaw cultural and language education and limited resources to meet it, Savvy decided to leave her government job and create her own company to do just that. In 2013 she launched Savvy UnLtd—with the UnLtd standing for "unlimited love to give." Initially meant to focus on motivational speaking, Savvy UnLtd's scope soon broadened to include #SpeakMikmaq, a movement that uses social media to teach, preserve, and encourage use of the Mi'kmaw language. Her company has allowed her to share these teachings around the world.

"Many youth are not growing up speaking our language," she said in 2014. "What we need is a Mi'kmaq language revolution."

Through #SpeakMikmaq, Savvy uses online skits that feature her speaking the language in everyday environments. In one, after chancing upon an old friend in a parking lot, she spontaneously explains how to say **pekwamuksin** ("it's nice to see you; long time no see"). Using her trademark upbeat and authentic approach, Savvy's #SpeakMikmaq platform amassed more than 45,000 followers at its height, quickly inspiring other communities to adopt similar hashtags, such as #SpeakMaliseet and #CreeSimonSays. She was named one of the "Top 40 Female Changemakers" in *Canadian Living* in 2015. Her platform's popularity also inspired her to launch an original clothing line. Worn by Savvy in many of her #SpeakMikmaq reels, Positive Vibes Only features Mi'kmaq words, symbols, and catchy quotes on clothing.

And while she has taken a pause from the spotlight in recent years to focus on raising her two boys, whom she began homeschooling in 2020, Savvy continues to channel her big spirit into those closest to her. In a public post she dedicates to her children on her @SavvyUnLtd Instagram account, she writes:

"To my sweet Divine Babies: May you always know where your roots come from… Your ancestors were freedom fighters who sacrificed so we can be here today…Celebrate your Indigenous wisdom, it's healing for the world & we have an abundance of it within us that we can access if we channel it. Know that you are a force to be reckoned with."

Inspired by the many L'nu'k and non-L'nu'k working to speak Mi'kmaw today, Savvy says, "If you learn, speak, or participate in our Mi'kmaw language and culture, wela'lin—thank you. Our ancestors thank you. It takes a whole village to keep us alive and every contribution matters."

CHEYENNE ISAAC-GLOADE
THE JINGLE-DANCING ENTREPRENEUR

Born: November 1989
Listuguj First Nation, QC

While she currently calls Millbrook First Nation home, Cheyenne Isaac-Gloade grew up on Quebec's Listuguj First Nation steeped in Mi'kmaw culture. The daughter of Vera Isaac and Dallas Morrison, she said she was already capturing attention jingle dancing along the powwow trail at just one year old. What's more, the entrepreneur learned to make a sale pretty young too. "When I was eleven or so, my grandfather made me sell cucumbers from our garden on the side of the road," she said, laughing. "I would sell them for 25 or 50 cents and make a little extra money. I think I even knew then I wanted to be an entrepreneur."

Excelling at the Mi'kmaw arts and culture classes offered at her Listuguj school, Cheyenne was just fifteen years old when she launched her first business, **Wasoweg** Creations (*wasoweg* means "flower"). Moving to Ottawa after high school, she gradually expanded her Indigenous network of craftspeople along with her technique, and eventually decided to enroll at the New Brunswick College of Craft and Design. After graduating from its Aboriginal Visual Arts program in 2014, Cheyenne transitioned Wasoweg Creations into Chey Designs. She met and married Garett Gloade of Millbrook First Nation a few years later. Garett eventually took the beading off her hands, when it became apparent they had

WHAT IS JINGLE DANCING?

Jingle dancing is performed by Indigenous women and girls at powwows to help heal and strengthen their people. The regalia worn for the dance is a jingle dress, which includes ornamentation with multiple rows of metal, such as cones, that create a cool jingling sound as the dancer moves.

become weak and arthritic from years of use. Sticking primarily to designing these days, Cheyenne's custom work and her husband's beading includes everything from regalia and jewelry to quillwork. And a fateful phone call from Los Angeles served to broaden the couple's skill set much further.

While working as an employee with Millbrook Youth Centre, Cheyenne took a call from Offsite Talent Agency. The talent agency was hoping to recruit Indigenous youth to audition for the set of a new music video. A tribute to missing and murdered Indigenous women, the video was set to the song "Powerless," written by Canadian musician Classified. Cheyenne helped rally youth for the video, and soon met Andy Hines, the agency's Nova Scotia–born director, on set. When Andy learned Cheyenne had made a red jingle dress herself to honour her husband's sister, a young Mi'kmaw woman who disappeared and has never been found, he was deeply moved. He asked her if she would do them the honour of wearing it in the video, and she agreed.

What began as an informal consultation soon blossomed into friendship, and within a few years, Andy, Cheyenne, and her husband joined forces to launch Project **Samqwan** (*samqwan* means "water"), an awareness campaign about the need for clean drinking water in Indigenous communities across Canada. With Andy leveraging his Los Angeles connections, he soon secured a Nike sponsorship, with the company donating several pairs of Air Force 1 Nike high tops for Project Samqwan bead designs. In the spring of 2021, the couple hosted their first sneaker-beading workshop at the Millbrook Youth Centre, where local Indigenous youth got busy transforming thirty pairs. While some bead pairs were later displayed at the Halifax Shopping Centre to raise awareness of Project Samqwan, a special children's pair was also designed by the couple with orange beads to read "215." This set was donated to the Tk'emlúps te Secwépemc First Nation memorial to honour the remains of the 215 Indigenous children discovered there that June.

And while they continue to broaden the scope of Project Samqwan, Cheyenne and Garett also recently collaborated with the alt-pop duo Neon Dreams on the set of their documentary series, *Illumination.*

"The fashion world, the music world, the film world—Indigenous people should and need to be there," Cheyenne said. "And that's something we want the youth to understand. That essentially being yourself and representing your culture can take you really far."

MAKAYLA BERNARD
SALES COME LATER

Born: 2008
Lennox Island First Nation, PEI

Makayla was around eight years old when she first started making art from traditional Mi'kmaw materials. She launched Quilling with Makayla after taking one quilling workshop on her Lennox Island reserve. She was just nine at the time.

"I decided I wanted to do something to make money," Makayla said. "My jewelry is made mostly from birchbark that I harvest myself and porcupine quills that I find in New Brunswick and Nova Scotia, as porcupines don't live on [Prince Edward] Island."

After collecting prickly porcupine carcasses with the help of friends and family, Makayla pulls and cleans the quills herself (which requires serious skill, by the way, if you want to avoid getting your hands pricked). "I start by soaking them in water with birchbark to make them easier to work with. [Next] I pull quills through the birchbark to create designs," she said. "Some I finish off with sweetgrass."

Makayla's family inspired her to dive into the traditional crafts scene and create her own business "sooner than most." Her family members, many of whom are craftspeople and entrepreneurs, began fostering Makayla's talents and ambitions when she was little. She said their support has been invaluable. They're still quick to jump in, whether to set up a Quilling with Makayla booth at a local market or just "stand in for the boss" on occasion.

With pieces ranging from elegant medallions, red dress–shaped earrings to honour missing and murdered Indigenous women and girls, framed eight-pointed stars, or handstitched quilts with a variety of Indigenous designs, Makayla said all her designs are Mi'kmaw- and nature-inspired.

Every holiday season since 2019, Makayla pitches in to support the Lennox Island Purse Campaign—a drive created to lend support to the women of her community. Harnessing her school community and Quilling with Makayla Facebook platform, Makayla rallies others to help her fill gently used and donated purses with quality items like perfumes, books, and various other purse-sized self-care products.

"I love fashion because it makes me look and feel really good and it makes other people look and feel really good, too," she said.

And when she's not busy with Quilling with Makayla or hanging out with friends, Makayla's on stage performing with Mi'kmaw Legends (a performance group), hosting quilling workshops for other up-and-coming artists, and on occasion, guest speaking at girls' empowerment retreats, teaching them how they can become entrepreneurs too.

She also sets time aside every year to do "something special" with her hard-earned money. For example, before returning to school in 2019, the then eleven-year-old used her summer sales money to buy the entire collection of the *Anne of Green Gables* book series.

While she hopes to continue making Mi'kmaw fashions for as long as she can, she does seem to have her priorities straight, as her August 2021 Quilling with Makayla Facebook comments demonstrate.

"I'll be at the powwow today, dancing. If you are looking for a pair of earrings, mom will have them with her. I feel like dancing is for me this year. Sales come later. #culture."

SELECT AWARDS

❋ Young Millionaires Award, the Lennox Island Development Corporation, 2019

❋ Award of Excellence, the West Prince CBDC, 2018

❋ West Prince Youth Entrepreneur Award, 2018

MI'KMAW GLOSSARY OF TERMS

The Smith/Francis orthography has 5 short vowels, a, e, i, o and u, and 5 long vowels, a', e', i', o', and u'. It has 11 consonants: j, k, l, m, n, p, q, s, t, kw, qw, and i can also act as a consonant. (When a Mi'kmaw orthography other than Smith/Francis is preferred by a particular L'nu, such as Listuguj, the authors have respectfully made note of their preference. We do this because we both understand and believe in practicing Etuaptmumk.)

Duwaken (due-wah-en): The Mi'kmaw game of ice hockey (as spelled by those L'nu'k who use the Listuguj orthography).

Epekwitk (eb-eh-gwitk): This translates to mean "lying in the water," and is the name for the area known as Prince Edward Island.

Epekwitnewaq (eh-be-gwit-nu-ah): Of or from Prince Edward Island.

Eskikewa'kik (es-gig-eh-wah-gig): The translates to mean "skin-dresser's territory," and encompasses Guysborough and Halifax County, Nova Scotia, and all the land and water in between.

Etuaptmumk (eh-do-up-tm-amk): Coined by Mi'kmaw Elder Albert Marshall, an Indigenous concept that means the inclusion and integration of multiple ways of knowing into a worldview and belief system, as opposed to just one. It is also known also as "Two-Eyed Seeing."

Glmuej (gl-am-oo-wech): This translates to "the one that sings before she bites you," and is the Mi'kmaw word for mosquito.

Keptin (gep-dn): Captain

Kespek (guess-beg): This translates to mean "the last land," and includes all the land and rivers north of Richibucto in New Brunswick, as well as the parts of Gaspé, Quebec, that connect to New Brunswick.

Kespukwitk (guess-boo-gwitk): This translates to mean "the last flow," and encompasses the communities of Queens, Shelburne, Yarmouth, Digby, and Annapolis in Nova Scotia.

Kitbu Amalkewinu (gid-bu amal-kew-inu): Eagle Dancer

Kji-keptin (gji-gep-tn): Grand Captain

Kopit (go-bit): Beaver

Ktaqmkuk (kta-um-gook): This translates to mean "across the water," and refers to the entire island of Newfoundland. It does not include Labrador.

Kulaman ma wanta'siwk (goo-la-mon maw wan-taw-siwk): Lest we forget

L'nu (el-new): One Mi'kmaw person

L'nu'k (el-noog): A group of Mi'kmaw people

L'nuey (el-new-way): Belonging to the people

Mawio'mi (mauw-wee-om-me): Formal gathering

Mawio'mi'l (mauw-wee-om-meel): The plural of Mawio'mi

Migitjo (mee-kee-choo): Grandmother (as spelled by those L'nu'k, like Savvy Simon, who use the Listuguj orthography)

Mi'kma'ki (mee-kmaw-gee): The area also known as Atlantic Canada, including parts of Maine and Quebec.

Mi'kmaw (mee-gmaw): An individual who is Mi'kmaw. The singular form of Mi'kmaq. Also used as an adjective when preceded by a noun, i.e. "Mi'kmaw rights." *See also L'nu.*

Mi'kmaq (mee-gma): A group of Mi'kmaw people; the entire Nation, i.e., "the Mi'kmaq Nation." *See also L'nu'k.*

Minuitaqn (min-oo-we-tah-qn): Recreate

Mimikej (mee-mee-gech): Butterfly

Msit mijua'ji'j kesite'tasit (em-sit mich-oo-wa-cheech kes-ee-teh-ta-sit): Every child matters

Netukulimk (ned-oo-goo-limk): This is an essential concept of the Mi'kmaq that grounds each person in an equally responsible, interconnected web of relationships between all living and non-living things on the planet.

Nikmaq (ni-gmaq): My kin or my friends

Pe'kwamuksin (bay-gwam-ook-sin): "It's nice to see you."

Pekwamuksin (bay-gwam-ook-sin): "It's nice to see you" (as spelled by those L'nu'k who use the Listuguj orthography).

Piktuk (bik-took): This translates to mean "the explosive place," and is the area also known as Pictou County.

Pu'tu's (poo-toos): These are the individuals appointed to keep the wampum belts, record the Mi'kmaw Grand Council meetings, and handle negotiations with any non-L'nu, such as treaty negotiations with colonials or disputes with other Indigenous tribes.

Qalipu (ga-lee-poo): Caribou

Samqwan (sum-gwun): Water

Sante' Mawio'mi (sawn-teh mawee-oh-mee): The Grand Council

Saqamaw (sa-a-maw): Chief

Segewa't (seh-geh-waat): To rise

Siawi-l'nui'sultik (see-ow-ee-el-noo-ee-sool-tik): "Keep speaking the language"

Sali'j (saw-leej): Sarah

Senetl (sen-a-tl): Senator

Senit W'jit Kanata (sen-it oo-chit ka-na-ta): Senator of Canada

Sikniktuk (see-gun-ik-took): This translates to mean "drainage area," and includes Cumberland, Nova Scotia, as well as the communities of Westmorland, Albert, Kent, Saint John, Kings, and Queens Counties, New Brunswick.

Sipekne'katik (see-peg-un-aye-ga-teeg): This translates to mean "wild potato area," and includes the City of Halifax as well as Lunenburg, Kings, Hants, and Colchester counties, Nova Scotia.

Sma'knis (smaw-gnis): Indigenous warrior

Sma'knisk (smaw-gnisg): Sma'knis warriors (plural); a collective of Indigenous warriors

Tepaqn (teh-bah-an): To drag along the ground, or the Mi'kmaw word equivalent of *toboggan*

Tu'aqn (tu-an): The Mi'kmaw game of ice hockey

Ulnoowe'g (el-noo-egg): Broadly translated, it means "to make indigenous or to adapt beliefs and customs of the Mi'kmaq." (Note that the organization Ulnooweg uses a slightly different spelling.)

Unama'kik (oon-a-maw-gig): This directly translates to mean "foggy lands," and refers to the area currently known as Cape Breton Island, NS.

Waltes (wall-tess): A traditional and ancient dice-and-bowl game played by the Mi'kmaq. Rumoured to be favoured by the Spirit World, it was temporarily outlawed by the Canadian government.

Wasuwek (wah-soo-wek): Flower

Wasoweg (wah-so-wek): Flower (as spelled by those L'nu'k who use the Listuguj orthography)

Wela'liek (well-aw-lee-ek): Thank you (when two or more people thank an individual or a group of people)

Wela'lin (well-aw-lin): Thank you (when one person thanks a single individual)

Wela'lioq (well-aw-lee-oh): Thank you (when one person thanks a group of people)

BIBLIOGRAPHY

Introduction
Nova Scotia Museum. "Spelling of Mi'kmaq." Accessed April 2, 2022.
  novascotia.ca/museum/mikmaq/?section=spelling

ACTIVISTS AND HEROES
Quotations
Googoo, Maureen. "Remembering William Basque, the Mi'kmaw veteran
  behind the poem, Sma'knis." *Ku'ku'kwes: Independent Indigenous
  News*, November 8, 2019. kukukwes.com/2019/11/08/remembering-
  william-basque-the-mikmaw-veteran-behind-the-poem-smaknis

Cape Breton University. "On Reflection." Accessed October 22,
  2022. cbu.ca/indigenous-affairs/mikmaq-resource-centre/
  mikmaq-resource-guide/on-reflection

Moore, Angel. "Mi'kmaq grandmothers give gas company eviction
  notice." APTN National News, March 12, 2019. aptnnews.ca/
  national-news/mikmaq-grandmothers-give-gas-company-eviction-
  notice

Sma'knis Sergeant Sam Gloade
Raddall, Thomas. "Sam Glode: Travels of a Micmac." *Cape Breton's
  Magazine* 35, January 1984, pp. 26-27.

Sma'knis Sergeant Wilfred C. Basque
Wentzell, Brittany. "Women start new tradition to honour Eskasoni's
  veterans." CBC News, November 11, 2019. https://www.cbc.ca/news/
  canada/nova-scotia/eskasoni-veterans-banners-1.5352689

Googoo, Maureen. "Remembering William Basque, the Mi'kmaw veteran
  behind the poem, Sma'knis." *Ku'ku'kwes: Independent Indigenous
  News*, November 8, 2019. kukukwes.com/2019/11/08/remembering-
  william-basque-the-mikmaw-veteran-behind-the-poem-smaknis/

Saqamaw Noel Geddore

Jeddore, Roderick Joachim. "Investigating the Restoration of the Mi'kmaq Language and Culture on the First Nations Reserve of Miawpukek." Masters thesis, University of Saskatchewan, 2000.

Jeddore, John Nick. "Forced to leave: The story of a Mi'kmaw forced into exile, as told by his great-great-grandson." *The Independent*, September 8, 2011. theindependent.ca/traditional-voice/forced-to-leave/

Saqamaw Oliver Lebobe

Fitzroy, Sir C. A. and Lord Glenelg. Sir C. A. Fitzroy's despatch to Lord Glenelg. *Colonial Office and Predecessors: Prince Edward Island Original Correspondence*, vol. 56, 1838, p. 168.

Kji-keptin Gabriel Sylliboy

Thomson, Aly. "Mi'kmaq leader gets pardon, apology from NS: 'He was the first to stand up for us.'" Global News, February 16, 2017. globalnews.ca/news/3253994/mikmaq-leader-to-get-pardon-apology-from-ns-a-man-of-great-significance

Government of Canada. Treaty Texts: 1752 Peace and Friendship Treaty Between His Majesty the King and the Jean Baptiste Cope. Transcribed from *R. v. Simon*, Supreme Court of Canada, 1985. Accessed November 7, 2021. rcaanc-cirnac.gc.ca/eng/1100100029040/1581293867988

Conn, Heather. "Sylliboy Case." *The Canadian Encyclopedia*, April 5, 2018. thecanadianencyclopedia.ca/en/article/sylliboy-case

Nova Scotia. Premier's Office. *Pardon, Apology, for Late Grand Chief Gabriel Sylliboy.* Office of the Premier, February 16, 2017. novascotia.ca/news/release/?id=20170216004

Elder Rachael Mary Marshall

Benwah, Jasen Sylvester. "This Month in History: August." The Benoit First Nation. Accessed Oct 1, 2021. benoitfirstnation.ca/august_month.htm

Barker, Salome. Alan Syliboy Interview. *The Xaverian Weekly*, June 30, 2018. xaverian.ca/articles/2018/6/30/alan-syliboy-interview

Donald Marshall Jr.

Martin, Sandra. "The life and death of Donald Marshall Jr." *The Globe and Mail*, August 6, 2009. theglobeandmail.com/news/national/the-life-and-death-of-donald-marshall-jr/article4283981

Lambie, Chris. "Donald Marshall Jr., 55: Fought racism, made history." *The Star,* August 7, 2009. thestar.com/news/obituaries/2009/08/07/donald_marshall_jr_55_fought_racism_made_history.html

Demont, John. "Donald Marshall Jr's enduring legacy." Op-ed. *The Saltwire Network,* October 23, 2018. saltwire.com/nova-scotia/opinion/john-demont-donald-marshall-jrs-enduring-legacy-512950

Elder Dorene Bernard

Dorene Bernard, interview by authors, Zoom.us, November 15, 2021.

Devet, Robert. "Mi'kma'ki Water Symposium is all about giving thanks and sharing knowledge." *The Nova Scotia Advocate,* October 6, 2016. nsadvocate.org/2016/10/06/mikmaki-water-symposium-is-all-about-giving-thanks-and-sharing-knowledge

Elder Lorraine Whitman

Lorriane Whitman, interview by author Robin Grant, Zoom.us, December 2, 2021.

Whitman, Lorraine. "Alter police practices now for Indigenous women's sake." Op-ed. *The Saltwire Network*, June 23, 2020.

Dr. Pam Palmater

Dr. Pam Palmater, interview by author Robin Grant, Zoom.us, November 17, 2021.

Palmater, Pam. "United Nations formally calls on Canada to respect and protect rights of Mi'kmaw fishers and prevent further violence." Pam Palmater's website, May 9, 2021. pampalmater.com/2021/05/united-nations-formally-calls-on-canada-to-respect-and-protect-rights-of-mikmaw-fishers-and-prevent-further-violence

Landyn Toney

Landyn Toney and Marsha McClellan, interview by authors Julie Pellissier-Lush and Robin Grant, Zoom.us, December 9, 2021.

Moore, Angel. "Mi'kmaw youth's walk raises $36K for residential school awareness." *APTN National News,* July 7, 2021. aptnnews.ca/national-news/mikmaw-youths-walk-raises-36k-for-residential-school-awareness

ARTISTS

Quotations

Hollett, Michael. "Wolf Castle Leads a Fresh Wave of Indigenous Hip Hop Voices." *Next Magazine.* Accessed November 4, 2021. nextmag. ca/wolf-castle-leads-a-fresh-wave-of-indigenous-hip-hop-voices

O'Neal, Morgan. "Rita Joe, poet laureate of Mi'kmaw, dies." *First Nations Drum,* April 28, 2007. firstnationsdrum.com/2007/04/ rita-joe-poet-laureate-of-mikmaq-dies

Reynolds, Ardelle. "Mi'kmaw couple gets global attention from Nike partnership." *The Saltwire Network,* March 29, 2021. saltwire.com/ nova-scotia/news/mikmaq-couple-gets-global-attention-from-nike-partnership-569487

Elder Rita Joe

Musial Steele, Charlotte. "Rita Joe wages gentle war of words." *Halifax North,* January 1991, pp. 11-13.

Joe, Rita. "Wigwam to Order of Canada," in *Women of Courage: 15 Cape Breton Lives,* edited by Ronald Caplan, 19-24. Sydney: Breton Books, 2016.

Soosaar, John. "Gentle Persuasion: Mi'kmaw poet's words inspired many." *The Daily News,* March 2007.

Joe, Rita and Lesley Choyce. *The Mi'kmaq Anthology.* Halifax: Pottersfield Press, 1997.

Tristan Grant

Tristan Grant, interview by authors, Zoom.us, November 15, 2021.

Hollett, Michael. "Wolf Castle Leads a Fresh Wave of Indigenous Hip Hop Voices." *Next Magazine.* Accessed November 4, 2021: nextmag. ca/wolf-castle-leads-a-fresh-wave-of-indigenous-hip-hop-voices

Loretta Gould

Loretta Gould, interview with author Robin Grant, Zoom.us, November 17, 2021.

Gord Downie & Chanie Wenjack Fund. "About the Secret Path." Accessed May 15, 2022. downiewenjack.ca/our-story/secret-path

Elder George Paul

Sweet, Jennifer. "Meet the Mi'kmaw elder whose song has become an anthem for his people." CBC NB, June 22, 2021. cbc.ca/news/canada/ new-brunswick/george-paul-mi-kmaw-honour-song-1.6073885

Radio Canada. "How a Mi'kmaw song ended up on an album by world-renowned cellist Yo-Yo Ma." October 8, 2021. ici.radio-canada.ca/rci/en/news/1830244/how-a-mikmaw-song-ended-up-on-an-album-by-world-renowned-cellist-yo-yo-ma

Elder Alan Syliboy

Barker, Salome. "Alan Syliboy Interview." *The Xaverian Weekly*, June 30, 2018. xaverian.ca/articles/2018/6/30/alan-syliboy-interview

Bell, Cheryl. "Interview with Alan Syliboy." *Billie Magazine*, November 2017.

Rebecca Thomas

Rebecca Thomas, interview by author Robin Grant, Zoom.us, June 12, 2021.

Rebecca Thomas, interview by author Robin Grant, telephone, May 8, 2022.

Lethbridge News Now. "Organized rhyme: How Halifax's poet laureate became 'a change-maker'" *Canadian Press*, April 17, 2017. lethbridgenewsnow.com/2017/04/17/organized-rhyme-how-halifaxs-poet-laureate-became-a-change-maker/

Kehoe, Paula. "Poetic justice: Mi'kmaw activist Rebecca Thomas champions social change through slam poetry." *Kawartha Now*, February 5, 2019. kawarthanow.com/2019/02/05/poetic-justice-mikmaw-activist-rebecca-thomas-champions-social-change-through-slam-poetry

ATHLETES

Quotations

Levi Denny, interview by author Robin Grant, Zoom.us, January 27, 2022.

Everett Sanipass, interview with author Robin Grant, telephone, February 3, 2022.

Levi Denny

Levi Denny, interview by author Robin Grant, Zoom.us, January 27, 2022.

Everett Sanipass

Everett Sanipass, interview by author Robin Grant, telephone, February 3, 2022.

Chad Denny

Chad Denny, interview by author Robin Grant, Zoom.us, January 13, 2022.

Sara-Lynne Knockwood

Sara-Lynne Knockwood, interview by author Robin Grant, telephone, November 21, 2021.

Richard Pellissier-Lush

Richard Pellissier-Lush, interview by author Robin Grant, Zoom.us, November 9, 2021.

Davis, Tony. "Island football coach wins national Indigenous award for work on and off the field." CBC PEI, November 6, 2020. cbc.ca/news/canada/prince-edward-island/pei-indigenous-coach-win-nov-2020-1.5792188

Tasha McKenzie

Tasha McKenzie, interview by author Robin Grant, telephone, February 3, 2022.

EDUCATORS AND KNOWLEDGE KEEPERS

Quotations

Sable, Trudy. Interview with Alex Denny. Mi'kmaw Native Friendship Centre Archives. Accessed April 18, 2022. mymnfc.com/archive/alex-denny-interview

Knight, Dianne. *The Seven Fires - Teachings of the Bear Clan by Dr. Danny Musqua.* 1st Ed. Prince Albert: Many Worlds Publishing, 2007. As found in First Nation's Pedagogy Learning Resources. "The Learning Spirit" in "Comprehending and Nourishing the Learning Spirit." University of Saskatchewan, 2009. firstnationspedagogy.com/NourishingtheLearningSpiritResources.pdf

The Maritime Edit. "[EDIT] presents... The inspiring story of Chief Mi'sel Joe and Miawpukek First Nation." YouTube video, 7:53. September 20, 2021.

Elder Elsie Charles Basque

Paul, Daniel. "Elsie Basque: Mi'kmaw pioneer." *The Halifax Herald,* October 1995. danielnpaul.com/Col/1995/ElsieBasque-MicmacPioneer.html

Lawlor, Allison. "Mi'kmaq teacher Elsie Basque was a revered role model." *The Globe and Mail*, May 8, 2016. theglobeandmail.com/news/national/mikmaq-teacher-elsie-basque-was-a-revered-role-model/article29934335

Alice Mitchell

McDonald, Reverend Maurice. Rev. Maurice McDonald to Rev. John A. MacDonald, Indian Superintendent, September 13, 1915. Indian Affairs School Files. RG10 Vol 6026, File 57-2-1, part 1.

Alex Denny

Cape Breton University. "Tribute to Alex Denny English Version." YouTube video, 8:56. May 12, 2016.

Elder Daniel Paul

Daniel Paul, in person and recorded interview by author Robin Grant, Kjipuktuk, Mi'kma'ki, November 16, 2021.

Palmater, Pam. "Danny Paul - We Were Not the Savages: *Warrior Life Podcast*." YouTube video, 1:13:39. October 31, 2021.

Koshy, Sonia. "Daniel Paul celebrates the removal of the Cornwallis statue." *The Signal*, February 4, 2018. signalhfx.ca/daniel-paul-celebrates-the-removal-of-the-cornwallis-statue

Elder Bernie Francis

Sable, Trudy. Dr. Bernie Francis Interview with Dr. Trudy Sable, January 16, 1999. Trudy Sable Collection, Mi'kmaw Friendship Centre Archives, Halifax, Nova Scotia.

Chang, Arturo. "Is the bus alive? Depends where you are: A brief primer on the Mi'kmaw language." CBC PEI, November 21, 2021. cbc.ca/news/canada/prince-edward-island/pei-mikmaw-language-mikmaq-1.6254510

CityNews. "Mi'kmaq dub of animated film 'Chicken Run' helps keep Indigenous language alive," January 31, 2021. halifax.citynews.ca/nova-scotia-news/mikmaq-dub-of-animated-film-chicken-run-helps-keep-indigenous-language-alive-3309065

Saqamaw Mi'sel Joe

Saqamaw Mi'sel Joe, interview by author Robin Grant, Zoom.us, January 2021 as well as telephone interview, May 21, 2022.

The Maritime Edit. "[EDIT] presents... The inspiring story of Chief Mi'sel Joe and Miawpukek First Nation." YouTube video, 7:53, September 20, 2021.

Dr. Marie Battiste

Downeast. "Dr. Marie Battiste's Favorite Maine Place." Accessed March 13, 2022. downeast.com/our-towns/marie-battiste-favorite-maine-place/

University of Saskatchewan. "Indigenizing the Academy: Indigenous Perspectives and Eurocentric Challenges." YouTube video, 1:18:01, April 13, 2016.

Indspire. "Marie Ann Battiste." Accessed on March 13, 2022. indspire.ca/laureate/marie-ann-battiste-2/

Elder Gerald Gloade

Nova Scotia. Aboriginal Affairs. *Mi'kmaq Artist Lives His Culture.* Office of the Aboriginal Affairs, June 26, 2007. novascotia.ca/news/release/?id=20070626015

The FPS Channel. "Mi'kmaq History Month 2020 – Gerald Gloade – Posters." YouTube video, 1:28, February 18, 2022.

Jones, Colleen. "Gerald Gloade's nickel unveiled at Millbrook First Nation." CBC NS, November 2, 2016. cbc.ca/news/canada/nova-scotia/gerald-gloade-nickel-unveiled-millbrook-beaver-first-nations-1.3833210

Moore, Angel. "Proposed open-pit mine in Nova Scotia threatens traditional hunting grounds says Mi'kmaw chief." *APTN National News*, January 29, 2022. aptnnews.ca/national-news/purposed-open-pit-mine-in-nova-scotia-threatens-traditional-hunting-grounds-says-mikmaw-chief

The Honourable Jamie Battiste

Battiste, Jaime. "Today I was pleased to join Mi'kmaw Kina'matnewey to announce new, supplementary funding for their work revitalizing and teaching the Mi'kmaw language as part of our government's ongoing support of Indigenous languages." Facebook, February 9, 2022. facebook.com/watch/?v=366046041656663

Fraser, Jeremy. "Jaime Battiste becomes first Mi'kmaw MP after winning riding of Sydney-Victoria." *The Saltwire Network*, October 22, 2019. saltwire.com/nova-scotia/news/video-jaime-battiste-becomes-first-mikmaw-mp-after-winning-riding-of-sydney-victoria-366447

MacDonald, Michael. "Meet Jaime Battiste: Nova Scotia's first Mi'kmaq member of Parliament." *The Canadian Press*, October 22, 2019. globalnews.ca/news/6068695/meet-jaime-battiste-nova-scotias-first-mikmaq-member-of-parliament

TWO-EYED SEEING SCIENTISTS AND DIGITAL MEDIA TECHSPLORERS

Quotations

Jennifer Sylliboy, interview by author Robin Grant, Zoom.us, January 25, 2022.

Dr. Rob Johnson, interview by author Robin Grant, email, December 21, 2021.

Jordan Alexander, interview by author Robin Grant, Zoom.us, January 28, 2022.

Elders Murdena & Albert Marshall

Albert Marshall and their daughter Michelle Marshall, interview by author Robin Grant, Zoom.us, January 3, 2022.

Elder Marilyn Sark

Marilyn Sark, interview by author Robin Grant, telephone, November 16, 2021.

Chris Googoo

Chris Googoo, in-person and recorded interview by author Robin Grant, Kjipuktuk, Mi'kma'ki, November 19, 2021.

Palmeter, Paul. "Canadian astronaut takes Mi'kmaq basket to space station." CBC NS, December 3, 2018. cbc.ca/news/canada/nova-scotia/canadian-astronaut-takes-mi-kmaq-basket-to-space-station-1.4929965

Dr. Rob Johnson Jr.

Dr. Rob Johnson, interview by authors Julie Pellissier-Lush and Robin Grant, Zoom.us, December 10, 2021.

Hodd, Colin. "Dr. Rob Johnson, Canada's first Mi'kmaq physician." Dalhousie News, June 19, 2018. medicine.dal.ca/news/2018/06/19/dr__rob_johnson__canada___s_first_mi___kmaq_physician.html

Jennifer Sylliboy

Jennifer Sylliboy, interview by author Robin Grant, Zoom.us, January 25, 2022.

Jordan Alexander

Jordan Alexander, interview by author Robin Grant, Zoom.us, January 28, 2022.

CRUSADERS AND ENTREPRENEURS

Quotations

Indspire. "Bernd Christmas." Accessed January 8, 2022. indspire.ca/laureate/bernd-christmas-2

Reynolds, Ardelle. "Mi'kmaw couple gets global attention from Nike partnership." *The Saltwire National Network,* March 28, 2021. saltwire.com/nova-scotia/news/mikmaq-couple-gets-global-attention-from-nike-partnership-569487

Karen, Mair. "P.E.I. Mi'kmaq groups urged to consider social entrepreneurship." CBC PE, May 18, 2018. cbc.ca/news/canada/prince-edward-island/pei-first-nations-mi-kmaq-social-enterprise-employment-barriers-1.4667425

Elder Doreen Jenkins

Doreen Jenkins, interview by author Robin Grant, telephone, January 28, 2022.

Senetl Dan Christmas

Senator Dan Christmas, interview by authors Julie Pellissier-Lush and Robin Grant, Zoom.us, November 18, 2021.

Jenene Wooldridge

Jenene Wooldridge, interview by authors Julie Pellissier-Lush and Robin Grant, email, February 2, 2022.

Karen, Mair. "P.E.I. Mi'kmaq groups urged to consider social entrepreneurship." CBC PE, May 18, 2018. cbc.ca/news/canada/prince-edward-island/pei-first-nations-mi-kmaq-social-enterprise-employment-barriers-1.4667425

Bernd Christmas

Bernd Christmas, interview by author Robin Grant, February 7, 2022.

Indspire. "Bernd Christmas." Accessed January 8, 2022. indspire.ca/laureate/bernd-christmas-2

Mary Beth Doucette

Mary Beth Doucette, interview by author Robin Grant, telephone, November 17, 2021.

Savvy Simon

Sage, Amanda. "Savannah Simon, motivational speaker-entrepreneur-visionary." *Kickass Canadians*, February 2017. kickasscanadians.ca/savannah-savvy-simon

Rendell, Lewis. "Sage Against the Machine." *The Coast*, May 7, 2015. thecoast.ca/halifax/sage-against-the-machine/Content?oid=4635528

Simon, Savannah. "To my sweet Divine Babies: May you always know where your roots come from." Instagram, April 27, 2021. instagram.com/p/CQZ3McQADum

Cheyenne Isaac-Gloade

Cheyenne Isaac-Gloade, interview by author Robin Grant, Zoom.us, December 2, 2021.

Reynolds, Ardelle. "Mi'kmaw couple gets global attention from Nike partnership." *The Saltwire National Network*, March 28, 2021. saltwire.com/nova-scotia/news/mikmaq-couple-gets-global-attention-from-nike-partnership-569487

Makayla Bernard

Chaisson, Jacqui. "Ten Talented Islanders Under 20 to Watch." *PEI Living Magazine*, Summer 2021. issuu.com/peilivingmagazine/docs/peil_sum21_issuu/s/12551687

Carranza, Ernesto. "Young Mi'kmaq entrepreneur finds her passion for fashion." *The Saltwire Network*, December 11, 2019. saltwire.com/prince-edward-island/news/young-mikmaq-entrepreneur-finds-her-passion-for-fashion-386816

Bernard, Makayla. "I'll be at the pow wow today dancing." Facebook, August 8, 2021. facebook.com/Quilling-with-Makayla-1582190448577075

OTHER BOOKS IN THE SERIES

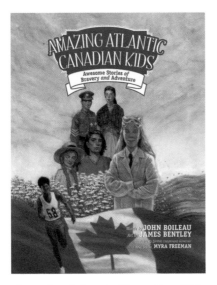

Amazing Atlantic Canadian Kids
ISBN: 978-1-77108-797-1

Amazing Black Atlantic Canadians
ISBN: 978-1-77108-917-3

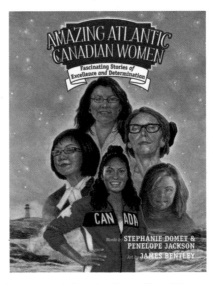

Amazing Atlantic Canadian Women
ISBN: 978-1-77471-016-6